HOW TO
START & RUN
your own
BED & BREAKFAST
INN

HOW TO

START & RUN

your own

BED & BREAKFAST

INN

• 2ND EDITION •

RIPLEY HOTCH & CARL GLASSMAN

STACKPOLE
BOOKS

Published by
STACKPOLE BOOKS
5067 Ritter Road
Mechanicsburg, PA 17055
www.stackpolebooks.com

Printed in the United States of America

10 9 8 7 6 5 4 3 2 1

Cover design by Wendy Reynolds

Library of Congress Cataloging-in-Publication Data

Hotch, Ripley.
  How to start your own bed & breakfast inn / Ripley Hotch & Carl
Glassman.– 2nd ed.
    p. cm.
  Includes bibliographical references and index.
  ISBN 0-81177-32231-2
  1. Bed and breakfast accommodations–Management. 2. Hotel
management. I. Glassman, Carl A. (Carl Averom), 1953– II. Title.

TX911.3.M27H6627 2005
647.94'068–dc22

2004027367

ISBN 0-8117-3231-2

Contents

Preface

More than a dozen years have passed since the first edition of this book was published, and much has happened to the inn business. For one thing, the explosive growth of the early 1990s seems to be over. Growth continues, but many fewer inns are being started from scratch, and many more are being bought as going concerns. We think this is healthy, so we have more to say in this edition about buying a continuing operation rather than starting one up.

Another important, but little discussed, change is lower occupancy rates. A decade ago, occupancy rates of 60 to 80 percent were not unheard of. A new survey from Michigan State University of several states shows that not only are occupancy rates lower, but they are lower than a lot of pundits would have you think. Rates of 30 to 40 percent are not unusual, even in established inns. Competition from more inns, and from midrange hotels and motels that offer more amenities, has made better marketing a top priority.

But better marketing is the promise of the biggest change since the first edition: the rise of the Internet. It was only beginning to be commercialized when this book was first written. Now it's the innkeeper's greatest friend—and in some ways, biggest danger. We'll have much more to say about it later on.

So, who are we, and what makes us worth listening to? Ripley Hotch has, with his partner Owen Sullivan, started three inns: Boydville Inn, in Martinsburg, West Virginia; The Inn on Montford, in Asheville, North Carolina; and now Biltmore Village Inn, also in Asheville. They used the advice in this book on both of those succeeding startups, and it works. We also have had the pleasure of hearing from a number of readers that this book has helped them avoid serious errors. We really do want our fellow innkeepers to succeed. Ripley has been an editor and writer for more than twenty-five years in newspapers and magazines, and he still works as editor of two business magazines for franchisors and franchisees. He also serves as adviser to the bed-and-breakfast program at Asheville-Buncombe Technology College. He holds a PhD in English from the University of California, Berkeley, and is the author of *How to Start a Business and Succeed.*

Carl Glassman is a co-owner and veteran innkeeper at Wedgwood Collection of Historic Inns in New Hope, Pennsylvania. Since 1982, he has offered how-to workshops and consulting services to aspiring innkeepers. In addition, Carl operates the oldest innkeeper apprenticeship program of its kind in the United States.

Carl and his wife, Nadine (Dinie), are raising their daughter, Jessica, born in 1994, while successfully growing their inn to include several adjacent historic buildings that cater to both leisure and business travelers, as well as the small meeting and event markets. A licensed realtor and management consultant, Carl is an adjunct professor of hospitality programs at New York University and the University of Delaware. He founded and served as president of the first regional and statewide inn associations in Pennsylvania. Carl holds a MSW degree in policy and planning from Rutgers University and is a frequent contributor to national inn and travel publications.

In this edition, we have made some corrections and additions, and have completely rewritten the financial, technology, and marketing sections to reflect current conditions. We're fully aware that this will change, probably tomorrow, but that's life.

We've been pleased to hear from readers over the last decade, and we encourage you to write one or the other of us or visit our weblog, naturally called "How to Start and Run Your Own Bed and Breakfast Inn," at http://bbstartrun.blogspot.com/. We also encourage you to read other books, take a seminar or two, and do extensive research on the Internet. Sleep around at other inns, and ask lots of questions of other innkeepers too; not only is this educational and fun, but it also may be tax deductible!

---- ◆ ----

Acknowledgments

One of the great delights in writing this book has been talking to innkeepers and the professionals who serve them. Innkeepers are a special breed. Even though we approached some for interviews during their busy season, the overwhelming majority gave generously of their time and advice. How generous, only fellow innkeepers can really know. Innkeepers are constantly being asked by guests about how to get into the business, and it can be wearing.

In spite of that, our fellow innkeepers went over what is for them the old, familiar ground and did it as if for the first time. That alone reconfirms the reputation of warmth, generosity, and sharing that all travelers associate with the time-honored term *innkeeper.* We've mentioned as many of our fellow innkeepers as we could in these pages, but we have inevitably left some out where others covered the same ground. Having a number of innkeepers say the same things was important to us; it confirmed trends and general advice. So to those we didn't mention, we also give our thanks.

Many of the folks we quoted in the first edition of this book are long out of innkeeping. (Not many have stayed with it as long as Carl and Dinie, but those who have are doing very well indeed.) What they said, however, is still good advice, so we haven't replaced them with others who would say the same thing. We have added a few here and there.

Some innkeepers are simply fantastic at what they do. You'll see them quoted rather more often than others. These people are truly awesome in their generosity, energy, intelligence, foresight, and creativity. In any other profession, they would be well paid. It's a tribute to them and to this peculiar business that these innkeepers feel well paid even when they bank very little or nothing.

So we offer a special thanks to the network of professional innkeepers, both the seasoned pros and the novices, for their enthusiastic support, encouragement, and assistance. I have to thank two old friends and coauthors of other books, Meg Whittemore and Michael Barrier, for some interview assistance. Both are avid inn-goers. They talked with several innkeepers on their visits with our question list and brought back the results. This enriched the final product. Ripley's brother, Kim, also contributed his unique perspective from Alaska.

We also owe thanks to the many wide-eyed aspiring innkeepers we have met through our seminars and other workshops. Most are now not only successful innkeepers, but also leaders in their state and regional associations.

Thanks also to Stackpole editor Kyle Weaver, who saw the need for a new edition of this book and set the wheels in motion.

A special thanks from both of us to our families, partners, and staff for covering for us during high season while we worked furiously to complete this project—both times.

Introduction

Welcome to one of only two professions in which you sleep with your customers. If one of them is the world's oldest profession, innkeeping—regardless of however many other professions have made the claim—must be the second oldest.

Some professions or callings seem to have an irresistible romance to them—astronaut, painter, poet, Olympic athlete, Supreme Court justice. But for most of us, these ambitions are beyond reach. We generally settle for amateur status.

Two other romantic callings seem more in reach: owning a restaurant and being an innkeeper. An astonishing number of otherwise sane people express a desire to do these, and a surprising number give one or the other a try, in spite of the fact that restaurants fail more often than any other business and innkeeping is notoriously low paying. Why do people still want to try it?

The romance of our caring profession may come in part from a delight in being onstage. Innkeeping is a form of theater in which you create the settings and star in the performance. You dream of being the perfect host with the perfect home. You assume you will be entertaining and expansive, a raconteur and guide. When guests like what you do, you get something very close to the glow performers get when they are warmly applauded. You think about the graciousness of the lifestyle and its relative freedom (working at home! no more going to an office! all that space!). Your inn is your castle, your kingdom, your baby, your profession, and your lifestyle. What could be more perfect?

Well, when something seems too good to be true, it probably is. That's not to say that innkeeping can't be a great life; it can. But it can also be very tough. The word most often used by innkeepers to describe their work is "confining." And they hadn't really expected that. They are able to have everything at home, but they can't get away from it. They have to be there to answer the phone (it might be a reservation) or to take care of an arriving or departing guest. Maintenance, visits from inspectors, the week's baking, and any number of other things limit the innkeeper's freedom.

For those who feel the draw of innkeeping, however, there is no discouraging word. Its pull can be almost overwhelming. For some of us, there is simply no way to avoid giving it a try.

You are probably one of those. In that case, nothing we say will discourage you, so we won't even make the attempt. Read this book and several others, and follow some of their advice. You'll have a better chance of success.

Two things are essential to creating a true inn: You—the owner—must be present as a host, and you must run it as a business. If you're interested in doing this as a hobby, that's fine, but you're running a bed-and-breakfast home, not an inn. If you're an absentee, then you're an owner but not an innkeeper.

If you're about to take up innkeeping, you'll find a lot of people willing to give you advice. That's what we're doing here. Innkeepers, however, are not always open to advice. All of us who have struggled into the business are opinionated. We often speak in absolutes, as if there were only one way to do things. We don't much like criticism, either, because we have so much of ourselves invested in our businesses.

We advise you to read other books, get more ideas and opinions, and talk to other innkeepers yourself. And we advise you to be careful about listening to people who have never kept an inn. It's not that they don't know useful things so much as that they simply do not have a sense of what is possible. Going outside the innkeeper circle is good for financial projections, accounting, and legal advice. But when it comes to what amenities you should offer, how to handle guests, how to create ambience, and above all, how much you can do, go to the folks who have been there. They are the ones who can give you a real feel for innkeeping.

We've gathered the best information we can from innkeepers and those who serve the business—analysts, former innkeepers, online marketing experts, insurance agents, lawyers, real estate agents, general business advisers—so that you can know what to do and in what order. If you follow this book almost like a recipe, you will have a better than fighting chance of success.

You'll find other books on starting inns, but many are written either by writers who have never been innkeepers or by former innkeepers whose experience and point of view are limited to their own inns. Although these resources also are valuable, we are offering advice based on interviews with many different innkeepers and service professionals from all regions of the United States and Canada. This approach will give you a real sense of the variety in this business. There are so many different ways of being successful that you should not think there is only one way of doing it right.

On the other hand, some standard ways of going wrong are common to all innkeepers. To succeed, we all agree that some things must be avoided.

You must be willing to change some of your most cherished plans, if necessary. You may have to make some decisions and compromises you do not like. You also have to be willing to make changes as you go along, because the world does not stay the same. Both the original version of this book and this revision were written in very difficult economic times, and some innkeepers are feeling the pinch, but many more are expanding and succeeding because they have altered their methods to fit the circumstances.

In fact, recessions, which hurt other businesses, can be a help to inns that cater to people taking short trips. During a recession, travelers cut down on longer vacations and take more quick getaway holidays—the inn's specialty. Both of our inns, Wedgwood and Biltmore Village Inn, have significantly increased business during these hard times, so don't let the doomsayers discourage you. Circumstances do control a lot of your life, but opportunity favors those who are prepared.

This book is arranged to give you an overview of the

innkeeping business and details of the steps you should take to create a functioning business. This will allow you to enjoy being an innkeeper instead of worrying whether business has been properly taken care of.

When business has been taken care of, you can take the innkeeper's special pleasure in listening to guests praise your inn and your hospitality. As Owen said one cold, slow March Sunday when we had ushered out the only two guests of the weekend, "When someone likes the inn that much, it makes it all worthwhile." If you can take pleasure in such intangibles, then this may be the job for you.

1

The Inn Business

The inn business is not small. There are no certain estimates, but a good guess is that the United States has more than 25,000 bed-and-breakfast inns, country inns, and homestays. Another measure is an estimate of rooms rented annually: at average rates of occupancy, approximately 15 million for inns. Contrast that with the 10 million rentals in 1991 for Best Western, the largest North American motel chain, with 3,300 properties.

Another measure is the number of sole proprietors. According to *American Demographics* magazine, about 10 million Americans work in their own unincorporated businesses. The largest number are in services (30 percent), and the largest number of those—321,000—are in lodging places: bed-and-breakfast inns, boardinghouses, trailer parks, camps, and "similar residences."

As it grows, the business is becoming more professionalized. What was once a random collection of guest houses is emerging into a field that has professional associations and an increasing interest in standards. Now, more than ever, it is important for new innkeepers to be armed with much more information than those in the vanguard had.

The opening and maturing of the inn business was much like the settling of the Old West. It started with generally unsettled territory and a notion that something was "out there." Then came the pathfinders, the few brave souls who started letting rooms in their houses after all the tourist homes of the 1940s and 1950s were displaced by the genius of Kemmet Wilson, founder of Holiday Inns.

Then there were the pioneers, who had a better notion of what they wanted to be doing. They started the small inns that Norman Simpson first wrote about in the 1970s in *Country Inns and Back Roads.* Then came the homesteaders like Carl and Dinie in the late 1970s and the settlers like Owen and me in the mid-1980s. When Laura Ashley starts creating signature inns and when Relais et Chateaux (the international luxury chateau–country house hotel chain) expands into North America, then our business is no longer a cottage industry.

So it's a good idea to begin with a description of what we mean by the term *inn* (corrupted from use by so many joints) and an examination of the trends in this diverse and burgeoning field.

DEFINITIONS

There's a good deal of argument—not always friendly—about the terminology used to describe inns. We'll start with the generally used terms and their ordinary meanings:

Bed-and-Breakfast Home

Also called a *homestay* or *host home,* this is a private home run part-time by its owners for a little extra money or as a way to meet people. It is the closest to the English bed and breakfast and was the start of the whole business in the United States. Small B&B homestays can be as professionally run as any full-service inn, but they are basically homes with an extra room where you stay cheek-by-jowl with the family. Breakfast is included and often served with the family. Homestays do not have a business sign and often are not regulated. Their business comes through overflow referrals from inns or bookings from a reservation service. For a commission, these services market and book reservations, often abiding by strict guest profiles provided by the hosts, such as "nonsmoking Christian motorcyclists" or "married couples with an interest in opera."

Bed-and-Breakfast Inn

This is the professionally run four to eighteen-room inn in which the owner-innkeeper is resident on the property (or very close by) and considers herself or himself to be a professional innkeeper. There may be assistant innkeepers, but the main contact of the guest is with the owner. B&B inns are usually historic or architecturally interesting buildings and are considered legitimate businesses. They have zoning board approval, collect sales and occupancy taxes, have use and occupancy permits, and maintain commercial insurance coverage. Breakfast is always included, though it may be continental, and there is a public gathering space for guests. B&B inns are regulated, often quite heavily, by state and local laws.

Country Inn

Also called *full-service inns* or sometimes just *inns* (surely you didn't think we were going to make this easy), country inns range in size from five to twenty rooms and can be in the city as well as the country. The country inn has a restaurant that serves meals other than breakfast. Breakfast may not be included in the rate, though it usually is. Because of the restaurant, and often a bar, these are the most heavily regulated of inns.

Other Types of Lodgings

Anything larger than about twenty rooms we regard as a small hotel, though small hotels can be as elegant and charming as a B&B or country inn. We do not believe, however, that it is possible for an innkeeping couple to maintain the ambience of an inn with more than twenty guest rooms.

Other niches exist among these categories, such as *historic inns* and *country house inns*. Bernice Chesler, one of the first guidebook authors, was often called America's bed-and-breakfast ambassador. Bernice died in 2002, and she'll be missed, especially by those veterans who knew her. She used to say that B&B owners are "very sure of what they do and how they're different. But the traveler really doesn't care about definitions. They care if you are a home or an inn." Beyond that, you'll have to explain the subtleties.

Throughout this book, we are talking about bed-and-breakfast inns as defined above, and our intention is to help you become an innkeeping professional. Even if you are interested in running a homestay or a full-service inn, however, much of the advice here will certainly be helpful.

TRENDS IN THE BUSINESS

The business is changing, and an aspiring innkeeper should be aware of a number of trends—some positive, some not. We'll come back to these in later chapters, but a quick survey of them is appropriate here. In the last twelve years, these trends have been continuing and strengthening.

Professionalism

"Innkeepers are becoming more professional—and that does not mean commercial," said Chesler. "We have reached the stage where it is a career for many, a primary source of income. Ten years ago, when they first started to blossom, the more common reason was for additional income and a certain lifestyle."

Cynthia La Ferle, former editor of *Innsider* magazine (unfortunately no longer published), says that more innkeepers are joining organizations intended to help them become more professional, and they're going to more workshops and seminars.

One simple indication of increasing professionalism is the number of inns listed in the yellow pages. According to the Professional Association of Innkeepers International (PAII), in 1989, there were 1,000 B&Bs and country inns serving one million guests. In 2001, there were 19,000, collectively serving 55 million guests annually.

Confusion among Hotels, Motels, and Inns

What is confusing to the traveler (and dangerous for the inn owner) is that many hotels and motels are calling themselves "B&Bs" and are putting in the kinds of amenities associated with inns, including an "innkeeper" who greets the guest. But that "innkeeper" is an employee with no stake in the business. We think this is confusing for travelers, who may never actually stay in an inn. And it makes marketing the real B&B inn much more difficult.

More Specialization in Style

As the market becomes more crowded and the inn traveler more discerning, it is important for you to know what kind of inn you want and how to project that to your potential guests. Cynthia La Ferle deplores the tendency of people to "jump on a band-wagon they know nothing about. We're getting stuck in a Victorian mode; that's well and good if you have a fine build-ing and you want it to be authentic." But there are other viable and attractive styles, she says. "Some are now doing English Tudor. Some are looking to the Arts and Crafts era, or the Mission era." For the most part, innkeepers go for the tradi-tional. According to PAII, B&B owners have renovated more historic buildings than any other industry segment.

As an aspiring innkeeper, you will have to think hard about the kind of inn you want. This goes beyond architecture. We have some suggestions for you in chapter 5.

Finding New Guests

Some inns are trying to appeal to business travelers. These trav-elers may like the inn environment, but they need certain things to conduct their business, such as telephones, desks, good light-ing, computers with Internet access, and fax machines. Many inns have added telephone jacks in rooms, but now suddenly everyone is bringing a cell phone and doesn't need your phone, thank you. Some inns (the Biltmore Village Inn, for example) had two lines going to each room so that guests could use their laptops and dial up their service. Recently, we added wi-fi (wireless fidelity), a wireless access point with fast Internet access from anywhere in the inn—and the telephone jacks may soon just be ugly patches on the walls. Being up-to-date techno-logically is a continuing battle, and some innkeepers have opted not to participate.

Sandra Soule, author of *America's Wonderful Little Hotels and Inns* and a regular columnist for BedandBreakfast.com, says that inns should consider appealing to children. Most inns do not; many even discourage children. But, she says, they're missing a bet.

Many innkeepers are marketing to single women traveling for business and pleasure. These women often find the home-like inn environment more comfortable, safer, and less threatening than a large steel-and-glass hotel. The ambience of an inn's parlor is a welcome alternative to the cold anonymity of a hotel lobby.

Over-fifty travelers are a market niche well worth reaching. Active retirees are probably going to be the fastest-growing travel group. They have the time for and interest in smaller inns, and they often travel midweek and off-season by preference. But they have their own special needs that the innkeeper must be aware of.

One fast-growing niche is the pet-friendly inn. A number of inns are finding this a lucrative market, and even high-end inns are setting aside a cabin, cottage, or room for pets. Some websites cater to this market, such as www.petfriendly.com. (More on children and pets at the inn in chapter 7.)

Other niches are business meetings, afternoon teas, weddings, banquets, and similar sorts of gatherings. For each of these, you must have an appropriate facility and a willingness to deal with special circumstances.

Inspections for Quality and Consistency
State and local regulatory agencies, local and regional inn groups, and travel associations are all tending toward more inspections. In the third category, the most famous are the Mobil Travel Guide and AAA. Both have included B&B inns in their programs for some time, under slightly different requirements than they impose on larger outfits. Their inspections include a strict series of requirements and end in a ranking.

Inn groups have a more informal inspection method. Since they are often associations of neighbors, the inspections can deteriorate into backbiting. Some associations have fallen apart because of feuding. Others, such as the Independent Innkeepers Association, organized by Norman Simpson and now known as Select Registry, have a base large enough that they can establish some standards.

There is a trend toward increased regulation by both the public and private sectors. Public policy concerns on the state level revolve around issues of health (food service and water quality) and safety (fire and panic). Local governments are concerned about maintaining the character of a neighborhood. Through zoning ordinances, they often restrict B&Bs by limiting the number of guest rooms and requiring a minimum size for lots and buildings, limiting the proximity of other B&Bs, and requiring off-street parking.

Private-sector regulations focus on a different set of qualities. Insurance companies want inns to be adequately covered for business interruption, product liability, and potential losses due to fire and theft. Automobile clubs, inn associations, and website guides are concerned with such "soft" standards as innkeeper presence, lightbulb wattage, cleanliness, and the quality of linens.

Carl recalls one memorable off-season midweek afternoon: "We had a state fire marshal inspect our inn for emergency exit signs, while a field inspector from AAA was investigating the adequacy of our interior window and door locks, and a potential house guest was bouncing on a bed mattress, checking its firmness! All three were 'unscheduled inspections' of very different, yet related, aspects of our inn. We passed all three, receiving a renewal of our use permit, a three-diamond rating from AAA, and a two-night walk-in reservation by the guest."

State and local regulations are becoming more detailed and, some innkeepers would say, more onerous. The positive side of this increased regulation is that it ensures a general upgrading of quality. And what is better for the business as a whole will certainly be better for individual inns. There's no question that we are all getting many first-time travelers, and one bad inn can lose a guest permanently. Regulations that prevent schlock operations from starting up, or that close some, are in every-body's interest.

On the other hand, regulations that are too picky destroy the delicate financial balance of inns. Many observers think that the larger motel and hotel industry would very much like to do this. That might be paranoia. Then again, it might not.

Changing Attitudes toward Rates

Bernice Chesler once remarked, when I complained about price resistance among travelers to rates that had not changed for two years, that there are always new travelers. New travelers in the late 1980s were not particularly sensitive to price. First-time inn-goers in the early 1990s, however, seemed inclined to resist rates they perceive to be too high. In the late nineties, boom times seemed to guarantee high rates forever. But today, price shopping is one of the favorite indoor activities of travelers. Travelers in the early 2000s seem to be looking for value as opposed to the luxury-at-any-price mentality that reigned in the 1980s and late 1990s. Private amenities—fireplaces, hot tubs, scenic views—do command higher room rates, but travelers are often looking for "affordable luxury." Still, a large segment exists for whom price is not an object, and who will regard severe price-cutting as a sign of lack of quality.

The Changing Vacation

Gone are the days when Mom and Dad packed Fido and their 2.3 children in a big station wagon and headed west for a two-week family vacation. Family lifestyles, economics, and work realities no longer permit such travel for many people. Since the realities of post September 11, even getaways close to home are being planned on extremely short notice.

The U.S. Travel and Tourism Administration has statistics that reveal a general trend since 1973 for Americans to take shorter, more frequent trips closer to home. The trend continues into 2006, according to the Travel Industry Association of America's 2005 report.

Extended weekend travel and midweek escapes within a one-tank drive of home now appear to be the norm. Gracious inns in historic, rural, or village settings are right on target. And as long as inns offer what many marketers call high touch—warmth and genuine hospitality, personal service, and attention to detail—to their guests, who live and work in an increasingly high-tech world, they will continue to grow and prosper.

Carl has noticed a corollary to this trend: the tendency of guests to roost in one spot and explore a region over several days. Day trips from the base might range as far as a hundred miles, from which the guests return "home" each evening.

This tendency is especially true of older travelers, who dislike having to find a different place to stay each night; worrying about whether they will like the next place as well as the last one, or wishing they had stayed longer, may spoil the day. Innkeepers can take advantage of this trend with clever marketing.

Upping the Ante

Rating systems and coverage in upscale publications and on websites are causing the public to expect a great deal of inns, particularly those in the luxury category. This is spilling over onto inns that have no such pretensions, as guests come to expect amenities that are expensive to provide and, in some contexts, ridiculous.

Ray Compton of Spring Bank in Frederick, Maryland, finds this trend depressing. "People are being led to believe that they need private baths, whirlpools, fax machines, fireplaces, telephones, televisions, king-size beds, and on and on. Ours is a historic house, and I'm trying to give people a feel of the past. There's wear and tear on the furnishings, but that shows it's close to the original." Many innkeepers actually try to discourage demanding guests from coming for fear that they may not appreciate the experience. On the other hand, meeting and exceeding high expectations is one of the great thrills of innkeeping.

This issue will be taken up in several places in this book. We suggest ways for you to create the kind of inn you want and then reach the kind of guest who will enjoy your house—without sending out false signals.

Innkeepers often create two major problems for themselves. One is the problem of honesty. Too many new innkeepers, buoyed by their enthusiasm, simply oversell. In the worst cases, they lie about what they provide or where they are located. This does a disservice to all other innkeepers. Heaven help you if you have done this and get a demanding guest. The unpleasantness of that experience is hard to match.

The second is a growing problem: the perception of public officials that innkeepers are likely to skirt the law whenever possible. We don't think this is true, but for reasons of expense, experience, time, and ignorance, innkeepers are sometimes unwilling to focus on the business and legal aspects of their new profession. They often keep very poor tax records or avoid getting permits.

Keep records from the beginning, either on paper or on your computer. If you're not good at it, then get a good bookkeeper or accountant. A certified public accountant who thinks about your business will often save more money for you than you will spend on him. Another reason to keep good records is that the IRS is beginning to do more audits of B&B inns, on the assumption that people are hiding money that they take in. That some inns have done so, combined with the poor tax records of honest innkeepers, has reinforced that assumption (bureaucrats do not like poor records).

We'll address both these problems in several ways as we go along. We don't think anyone is going to give you trouble if you are honest and know what laws and regulations apply to you.

More Food Service
More and more travelers expect an afternoon tidbit or to take an evening meal in the inn. We suspect that this trend will continue. Inns have a number of ways to approach this problem—or opportunity, depending on your perspective. One is to hire a

chef, build a commercial kitchen, hire a wait staff, and start taking dinner reservations. This is expensive. An up-to-code commercial kitchen costs upward of $50,000, a chef isn't cheap, and a wait staff is hard to manage. Add to that the liquor license and all the extra attention from various zoning, licensing, and taxing bodies, and you have a recipe for a headache. Other inns have exceptions that allow them to serve meals on a small scale or as part of a special prearranged package.

Another solution is to bring in outside caterers for specific meals. Trying food service on this scale will allow you to discover whether it is something you want to do and whether it is profitable. Catering is a clearly defined outside service; you're not doing any of it. The problem is that this cannot be done flexibly; you don't want to absorb the cost of uneaten meals that you ordered on speculation. And if you get into this in a large way, you're still going to need waiters. You'll also be pretty tired. Still, if you want something special for guests, you can offer prix fixe meals to groups of at least a certain size, guaranteed as your rooms are.

COMPARING US WITH HOTELS

When we compare ourselves with the hotel and motel industry, we aren't at as much of a disadvantage as you might think. We ought not to try to compete with the hotel-motel industry on price, because it invites the wrong kind of comparison and forces us toward unprofitability.

Hotels and motels often got financing from overgenerous banks in the 1980s, and they did not adapt well to the new realities of the 1990s. Some chains have gone into bankruptcy; others have sold out. In fact, things weren't so hot for the hotel industry even in the go-go 1980s. It ran up ten consecutive years of losses from 1981 to 1991—reaching losses of $1,000 per room for the year. Hotel occupancy rates dropped to 59.2 percent in 1991, and it dropped still further after the terrorist attack of September 11, 2001.

The economy segment and the all-suite segment of the hotel-motel industry have done better. They're the fastest-growing;

people are willing to cut down on frills to save money. The occupancy rates of those segments can be over 60 percent.

Hotels and motels are generally better run and smarter in the new century. They offer bed-and-breakfast-style amenities, such as newspapers, breakfast, whirlpools, Internet access, and cable TV, and are adjusting their rates to reach special segments. Nothing that we can think up will avoid their notice, and they'll imitate it if they see an advantage. That's just smart business.

What does this means for inns? 1) Our rates compare reasonably well to the industry as a whole, given that we don't have their marketing power. 2) Our guests really want to stay with us. 3) Be very, very careful about competing on price. As Dinie says, "Inns are an 'experience,' and a hotel-motel room is a commodity."

We are also much less leveraged; the full-service hotel-motel industry is being eaten alive by its debt service, because so many units were built. Over time, as the industry shakes out and there is less lending for lodging, the number of rooms will diminish, occupancy rates will go up, and we'll still be in fine shape in the inn business.

COMPETITION AMONG OURSELVES

It is probably inevitable that as inns grow more attractive as an alternative to the nine-to-five job, more people will be trying it than should. It just looks too easy. Arna Fay, who owns the Fox Creek Bed & Breakfast in Fox, Alaska, puts it succinctly: "Everyone in this area with an extra bedroom seems to think he or she can open a B&B, charge half what the hotels charge, brew up coffee in the morning, throw a couple of rolls on the table, and make lots of money. Greed and ignorance are creeping into the business."

This is a serious matter. A good part of the charm of this business has been the generosity of longtime innkeepers toward newcomers. Not only have many established innkeepers been willing to do seminars, whose price never covers the value given, but they also offer advice without charge as new innkeepers struggle with the inevitable bumps in the road. There are, however, exceptions to this rule. If it comes to a choice between saving the business and generosity to the innkeepers, the business is going to come first.

Some communities have experienced overbuilding, and the result is more concern in the community about how many B&Bs there are. Some inns have failed, and some have been turned back into private homes. That trend may continue as real estate values go up in many areas of the country.

Predators—people who trade on the businesses of those who do things right—are coming into the market. These people thumb their noses at zoning, health, fire, and safety regulations, and brazenly advertise on the Internet, pulling unsuspecting guests away from legitimate inns. Other nasty practices we have seen include guest stealing (referring guests when they are full, but keeping their names and calling back if they have a cancellation); misrepresenting other inns; and calling government agencies or regulatory groups such as AAA with anonymous accusations of lawbreaking in other inns.

People do strange things when they get desperate. We hope we can prevent some of these things from happening to the business by urging you to have a strong financial foundation, do good research, present a unique inn, and operate ethically.

2

Beginning at the Beginning

"PREDICTABLE PERSONS WORK FOR WAGES; UNPRE-
DICTABLE PERSONS ARE INNKEEPERS."
—Hugh Lineberger

Certainly it's true that innkeepers are unconventional. Says
Heinz Hailbach, former owner of the Millstone Inn in Cashiers,
North Carolina, "You have to be a little bit crazy to do this."
Dick Butkus, who with his wife, Ellen, owned and operated
Hollileif in Wrightstown, Pennsylvania, described us all very
well after a year of innkeeping: "A wonderful quality of innkeepers is that they are all, at least a bit, out of step with the
world. A great attraction of innkeeping is the ability to make
one's own decisions and choices. For the most part, innkeepers
are fun-loving, cheerful people. Perhaps the eccentricity of the
innkeeper is what makes each B&B a special place. A little
craziness can go a long way in making a weekend memorable."
The Butkuses have since sold their inn and retired.

WHO MAKES A GOOD INNKEEPER
Early on in our research for this book, Carl, Dinie, and I were
sitting at the breakfast table of the Scarlett House (recently
renamed the Kennett House) in Kennett Square, Pennsylvania,

after innkeeper Susan Ascosi had served us breakfast. We were speculating about who made a successful innkeeper, not in terms of the business end of things, but in terms of who really enjoyed the experience. Susan had been a nurse and an administrator, I had been a teacher, and Carl and Dinie were both in human services.

We talked about other innkeepers we knew and came to the conclusion—since confirmed by many interviews—that the good innkeepers had been in service professions, and often caregiving ones. Nurses (not doctors), salespeople, teachers, consultants (who are teachers of a sort), homemakers, and personnel professionals all seem to have what it takes to deal with guests. Indeed, like a true health-care professional, we often dispense tertiary mental health care to our houseguests, though we have yet to find insurance company reimbursement for our innkeeping services.

Innkeepers usually come in pairs (the lone innkeeper is fairly unusual), and the two partners complement each other in interesting ways. If one is a caring type, the other is often a business type. One is the maintenance person, the other the marketer. Various characteristics of the two may combine in unusual ways—but ways that work.

John and Maureen Magee, formerly of Rabbit Hill in Lower Waterford, Vermont, are a classic example. John was in life insurance, and Maureen was a teacher and administrator. "But John was a teacher before he was in life insurance," says Maureen. "In our careers and in life, we were serving people. We can now recognize that we love to take care of people." For an innkeeper, taking care of people means showing a kind of care that will surprise the guest. "We have aspiring innkeepers who come to us for advice, and we ask them why they want to do this. Some never mention the guests and never mention giving of themselves. But we need to ask ourselves continually what differentiates the hospitality we offer from that of a hotel or motel. That owner is not likely to sit in the emergency room with the guest who fell and broke an arm. We try to find the little unspoken thing that a guest needs and meet that need. A person who is continually coughing in the dining room might find a hot toddy or hot tea in the bedroom, and some Halls cough drops."

Sid and Judy Clemmer moved from Texas to Leadville, Colorado, to open the Leadville Country Inn in 1989. Judy had worked for more than seven years as the director of a day-care center with eighty-seven children and fifteen staff people. Sid had worked as a salesperson for his father, a Coca-Cola bottler, for years. Even though both thought Judy would deal more with the people side of innkeeping, it has worked out the other way.

Hugh Lineberger opened the Gastonian in Savannah, after a twenty-two-year career in temporary personnel work. Although his wife, Roberta, worked for a time in their agency, she was mostly a homemaker, raising five daughters. The Linebergers were over sixty when they opened the Gastonian from scratch. Hugh says that most innkeepers are older people. "Older people are more interested in love than money." He thinks of himself as a salesman. "It used to be a common saying in Savannah that if you shook hands with Hugh Lineberger, you had a brochure on the backswing. We sell all the time; that's what life is, it's selling."

The original owners of Old Yacht Club Inn in Santa Barbara, California, both were in education. Nancy Donaldson was a dean, and Lu Caruso was an assistant principal. One day Nancy came into Lu's office and said, "I'm sick and tired of chasing these kids around in my high heels. I have better things to do." Says Lu: "Nancy had done extensive traveling in Europe and always stayed in bed and breakfasts. She found this house and said the worst thing that could happen, if it didn't go, was that we would have an interest in a beautiful house near the ocean in Santa Barbara and enough rooms to accommodate all of us. So we said okay and gave it a whirl." Eventual success followed.

Nancie and Lee Cabana took over Brookview Manor in Canadensis, Pennsylvania, in July 1991. Lee had been an executive with the Red Cross, and Nancie was a recreational therapist. As new innkeepers in the Pocono Mountains, they quickly learned not to bowl over houseguests with their old credentials or job status. "From a guest's perspective," says Lee, "there are only two roles at an inn: the server and the servee. A good innkeeper appreciates that guests may not give a damn about his MA in English. They just want help in getting their luggage upstairs. Coming from the human services made the transition into the hospitality industry very easy for us."

People in these professions at least understand that they can deal with people and like it. These successful innkeepers come back again and again to what all of us who have done this know: You have to be able to be around people all the time. "If you love to have houseguests every day, seven days a week, and if you love to talk, repeating worn-out stories and answering nonsensical questions, then inns are for you," says Hugh Lineberger. Certainly a successful inn business is a lot more than the sum of its twenty-first-century high-tech components.

If you have not been in a people profession, at least do some soul-searching. As Bernice Chesler once said: "You will be associating with other people absolutely full-time. And for the successful innkeepers, that is one of the perks. They really do love people. The friends they make through the business are a major reward, one they were seeking in their previous profession and never found."

It seems, in fact, that most innkeeping partnerships have one member who was miserable, or at least unfulfilled, at the work he or she had before. That's the negative that pushes them into innkeeping, the flip side of the love of people that pulls them into it.

BECOMING AN INNKEEPER

There are three principal ways of becoming an innkeeper: get hired as one, buy a going inn, or start an inn from scratch.

Arline Stephan, former resident innkeeper at Wedgwood, is a good example of the professional staffer. She says she had all the motivations to be an innkeeper, "except that my husband had no interest in innkeeping, and neither of us had a strong desire to be self-employed." So she set out on a national job search and landed her position, in a place she likes and in an area where her husband could find work in his field.

For years, Annette King was an inn-sitter and consultant for inns from North Carolina to California to Rhode Island to Alaska. She says that she has no interest in the headaches of owning an inn, but she loves being an innkeeper. So although she hasn't the potential profit from ownership, neither does she have the burden of finding the money to keep one going.

King's Cottage, a seven-room B&B in Lancaster, Pennsylvania, employed a full-time nonresident innkeeper to provide support to former owner Karen Owens. Because her husband, Jim, was employed full-time outside the inn, Karen needed professional staff to help her run the inn. The staff also kept things running when they took their vacation.

More innkeeping positions have opened up as successful inns expand and the industry matures. Though it's not for everyone, working at an inn does have its advantages. Arline said of her former innkeeper job that although she processed the reservation deposit checks, she gave all the bills to Carl and Dinie, "one small example of enjoying the fun parts of innkeeping without the hassles of ownership."

The changing nature of the inn business makes our suggestions about becoming an owner now different from the ones we might have given fifteen or twenty years ago. When Carl started in 1981, there were not that many inns. When I started in 1987, there were enough for it to be considered a strong trend. Now there are so many that new inns have to work much harder to be noticed. And if you're not noticed, you'll never make it.

In chapter 4, we'll go into the details of both buying an operating inn and starting one from scratch; for now, we want to look at why you would choose one approach or the other. It's the most basic of your decisions—even before you decide you're going to be an innkeeper, because that one you can rescind up until the time you sign the closing papers.

If you start from scratch, many more of your decisions are going to be critical. You will have a great deal of work making sure that your licenses are going to be correct, or that you can get them at all. You will save the money of paying for a going business, but you will have to do much more work to assure there will be a business for you. Are you willing to be a pioneer in a new area? Do you have the stamina for writing (or rewriting) laws; working with contractors, lawyers, accountants, and others who have never dealt with inns; and finding the market—if there is one? (For more on this, look at chapter 4.)

If you buy another inn, you have to deal with the previous clientele, which may not be the kind you want. That was the case for John and Maureen Magee, who bought Rabbit Hill Inn as an ongoing enterprise. "We made our peace with the fact that part of the price was the existing clientele," says Maureen. That was not the kind of quest they wanted. "It was a family place, inexpensive and European plan, and we just gave that up."

Carl and Dinie bought a former rooming house and turned it into the Wedgwood Inn. They felt that having an already going business, even though a different one, was a help to them. When Sid and Judy Clemmer bought the Leadville Country Inn, it had been closed for a while, but they knew their licenses would be in place.

Owen and Ripley started Boydville from scratch; there wasn't even another inn in town to serve as a guide. They were the first with everything, and what they saved by not buying a previous business, they spent in agony and aggravation. The same was true when they started the Inn on Montford and, most recently, Biltmore Village Inn. Biltmore had been a B&B for some years, but its reputation was not what either of them wanted. Still, occasional guests from the old days call, and the old name still turns up a few inquiries.

You may be able to start from scratch with less hassle: Deb and Gary Leitner of Hillside Farm in Lancaster, Pennsylvania, had a large farmhouse with the potential for four to six guest rooms, two acres of grounds, a quiet rural setting, and a strong tourist area. They attended an innkeeping seminar, visited other inns, and had in Gary an important resource: He was an electrical engineer and could do all of the conversion work himself. They both kept their full-time jobs so that they could ease their way into innkeeping gradually.

Money and location can do wonders. Hugh and Roberta Lineberger started the Gastonian from scratch; they insist they wouldn't have done it any other way. But they spent a great deal of money—over $2 million—and the inn has a great location in Savannah.

Inheriting a piece of property or an old house is a good way to start—if you can arrange it. Dan and Darlene McNeill inherited the Inn on Providence in Charlotte, so it made sense for them to start their inn there. They made a great success of it. Now Charlotte has refused to allow new inns in the city limits unless they are grandfathered. Although this is shortsighted of the city, it gave the Inn on Providence a great advantage.

As more innkeepers retire from the business and commercial lenders become more restrictive, leasing a working inn has become a real option. The McNeills decided to leave innkeeping and put their property on the market. Joann Celani, who had opened an inn on her farm in Romeo, north of Detroit, wanted to buy it, as her husband was ready to retire from the cold weather. "It takes too long to start from scratch, so I wanted to buy an established one," says Joann. But the Michigan property did not sell, so Joann worked out a lease arrangement with the McNeills. "The only thing that was strange was walking into someone else's home. I felt like an intruder."

But, she says, it was just the thing to do. In Romeo, the farm was out in the country and didn't do much more than pay the insurance and provide a little spending money. "In Charlotte, we were paying our lease and paying our daughter [who was the assistant innkeeper], and we had cleaning help—and I was making money." Joann advises: "Buying a going proposition is the way to do it. All the licenses are in place, the brochures are done, you have a good reputation, you're in the books and online directories. Leasing is marvelous; what better way to find out if you like it?"

Joann wasn't able to sell the property in Michigan, however, and after a year, she decided not to keep the lease at the Inn on

Providence. The McNeills went back to innkeeping and decided not to lease again. Sometimes, especially when the real estate market is slow, leasing options are more available. When the market is tight, however, this is not true.

Eventually, the McNeills sold to a buyer who closed the inn altogether. The Inn on Providence is now a private residence— a trend that may continue in areas where real estate is hot.

Leasing often is not an option, but when it is, you might find it is just for you. Eventually you may be able to demonstrate to a bank that the property is doing well enough for you to finance the purchase out of earnings. For younger people without a large nest egg for a down payment, this can be the way into innkeeping.

Other, often complex, methods can make innkeepers out of people with less credit or means, but these require the advice of professionals, such as real estate agents, lawyers, accountants, and bankers. Don't give up when conventional routes don't get you there. If you really want an inn, there are ways to obtain one and people to help you find those ways.

WHAT YOU NEED BESIDES MONEY

Money is an obvious necessity for inn owners. We'll save money matters for chapter 4, but you should know that it exists in many forms and can be leveraged to go a long way.

Other extremely important assets for potential innkeepers include a good sense of humor and good health. As an innkeeper, you really are indispensable—ask innkeeping pairs how life is when one of them is too sick to move. If you are prone to illnesses or have a debilitating condition, don't consider innkeeping. Likewise, if you are not energetic and self-starting, stay away from this business. You should be the kind of person about whom others say, "I don't see how you do all the things you do." For most innkeepers, seventeen-hour days are routine. And they are hard days, full of physical activity, mental gymnastics, and psychological strain.

According to Dane Wells, former owner and innkeeper of the Queen Victoria in Cape May, New Jersey, for more than twenty-four years: "If you do it on a professional level, you're going to be working a seventeen-hour day, and you're going to be doing it seven days a week. You have to have a little streak of workaholism going through you to survive."

Innkeepers typically think they can do everything. Often they can. Here's a sample of recommended innkeeping skills: light carpentry, gardening, troubleshooting problems of old houses, using a computer, writing press releases, handling Chamber of Commerce committee work—all in addition to being a congenial host, of course. If you can do all this, you certainly have the skills to own an inn.

The mistake we all make is to assume that we can do it all at once. Time really is unforgiving, so you should also be the kind of person who knows his or her limits.

That's easy advice to give. When Carl and Dinie decided to renovate the third building in the Wedgwood Collection of Historic Inns, the Aaron Burr House, Carl put in eighteen to twenty hours a day on the renovation. A week after opening the inn, Carl contracted double pneumonia. Everyone who has been involved in a renovation project has pushed the limits, and that's okay once in a while, but you can't make a habit of it.

3

If You Don't Do Anything Else . . .

"THE MOST CRITICAL PIECE OF ADVICE THAT ANY-
BODY NEEDS IS TO UNDERSTAND THAT THE BED-AND-
BREAKFAST BUSINESS IS A BUSINESS."
—Murray Burns

We've spent a lot of time asking successful innkeepers what they did to ensure their success and what they would have done differently if they had it to do over. Surprisingly few said they would have changed their approach. But some rules emerged that you should take to heart. These rules won't keep you from failing, but they will form a safety net.

The rules are centered on taking care of details before you take the final step. You need to do as much advance planning as you can, because all hell breaks loose when you walk in the front door and take possession of your inn property. We'll look at some of the rules in depth here and will take up others in more detail in later chapters.

RULE 1: FIND A GOOD LOCATION
The most important rule in innkeeping is having a good location. How you define "good" depends in part on the kind of inn you want to have and the kind of innkeeper you want to be.

Certain locations offer good opportunities for inns: college towns, many national parks, major historic sites, midsize business destination cities, and getaway locations such as seashores and mountains. Not many places have all these qualities, and those that do are pretty well saturated. Each kind of location imposes different characteristics on inns located there.

College towns, for example, put you in the room-rental business, and price is a major consideration. Your guests will include parents visiting their kids, parents bringing kids to look at the school, football fans, concert-goers and performers, visiting faculty and lecturers, recruiters, and so on. Most of these people will be there for a specific purpose, and they will be looking for convenience at a reasonable price. Relaxation usually is not their goal.

National parks and *historic sites* bring you travelers interested in history and touring. These are often older guests, with plenty of discretionary income. They will be looking for special advice on how best to see the sights they have come for. Innkeepers need to be knowledgeable about the logistics for visiting the local attractions. Williamsburg, St. Augustine, and Gettysburg are examples of principal historic locations.

Newport, Rhode Island, is a typical coastal area with dramatic scenery and the added attraction of historic sites. It is so popular that it has more than a hundred B&Bs and homestays, and during the tourist season, four months of the year, every room in every establishment may be filled.

The Voss Inn is located in Bozeman, Montana, near Yellowstone Park. Innkeeper Bruce Muller says: "Yellowstone draws visitors from every state in the union, plus many guests from other nations. I think we have to know more about Yellowstone than the park rangers! Guests particularly like our driving instructions. We direct them on back roads through small towns to get there."

Favored *recreational locations* are oceans, lakes, and mountains. Outdoor activities such as boating, skiing, hiking, and bicycling draw visitors to these areas. These outdoorsy people are looking for more rustic inns as a rule, so if you plan to open an elegant place filled with porcelain and lace, avoid locations such as Vail, Colorado.

Mary Davies began Ten Inverness Way in Inverness, California, as a four-room inn located in a great hiking area near Point Reyes National Seashore. Although the inn now has new owners, it still retains the ambience she created in 1980. Mary told us when she had her inn: "I like for my guests to feel comfortable walking into the inn without first having to take off their hiking boots. I'm not a froufrou person and haven't decorated the inn that way. Most of our guests come to this area for outdoor activities, and they aren't froufrou people either. We keep on hand maps of the park and materials on bird-watching, horseback riding, and hiking trails. The books we sell in the living room also reflect these interests. We tend not to attract couples looking for a romantic escape."

One major trend among travelers is to take shorter vacations closer to home. The *weekend getaway* and the *midweek escape* are popular with harried city workers. Some areas have become tourist meccas, excellent getaways within a few hours' drive of major cities. Galena, Illinois, just three hours from Chicago or Milwaukee, is such a place, as are the Upper Peninsula and Mackinaw Island in Michigan. Another popular getaway destination is Bucks County in Pennsylvania, whose location within four hours of one-third of the U.S. population makes it a great home for inns. Urban escapees are often younger couples without children. These college-educated professionals look for upscale inns in country or village settings.

Galena, Illinois, is the location of Aldrich Guest House, an elegant Greek Revival house that offers five bedrooms. A Chicago native, innkeeper Judy Green left a New York City publishing career in 1985 to purchase the then-one-year-old fledgling B&B. The inn is her sole means of support, and she operates it seven days a week year-round, with only cleaning help and an occasional innsitter. More than 50 percent of her business is urban dwellers.

"I can usually spot a city couple by the car they're driving—often a late model, two-door sports car," Judy says. "They are often seeking a romantic spot or simply a place to relax from the stress of their corporate jobs. When they make reservations, they are happy to hear we don't have in-room telephones or televisions, and they are absolutely delighted that we have lace-canopied beds and bathrooms with pull-chain commodes and claw-foot tubs. They often take in some historic sightseeing and antique hunting and usually ask about reservations at the best restaurants. This is definitely a quality-conscious market, not a cost-conscious one."

Such areas can be very tough for aspiring innkeepers who plan to start from scratch, because acquisition costs may be high and those areas may be approaching saturation. They also may be at the mercy of gasoline prices and availability, since most guests reach their getaway destinations by car, not public transportation. If a getaway destination is reliant on one metro-politan area for most of its guests, the inn's business may be adversely affected by a regional economic recession.

If you find a developing destination of this kind, it can be a real opportunity if you have the financial resources to hold on while it matures. One problem for such areas is getting mid-week business. Boydville, for example, was located in a devel-oping getaway location, near two national historic parks, a good deal of recreation, and shopping. All the inns in that area have difficulty getting midweek business, though most have no prob-lems on Saturday nights. Obviously, filling all your rooms one night a week is never going to get you to 65 percent occupancy if that is where you need to be.

The U.S. Travel and Tourism Agency found that shopping has come to be a significant form of entertainment within the past couple decades. Outlet malls are attractive to many guests, not as the primary draw for your inn, but as one of many things to do in the area.

Business travelers have discovered inns and are filling them during the week. That makes *midsize cities* like Charlotte, San Diego, and Minneapolis good potential locations. Such cities often have restrictive zoning, however, limiting inns to historic areas or to a maximum of two rooms, which dooms a serious professional innkeeper. They also have the opposite problem of tourist destinations: They can be hard to fill on weekends.

Urban inns often have an entirely different clientele with very specific needs. They usually attract single businesspeople who require convenient locations for doing business. An urban inn must provide telephones, televisions, and now wi-fi, high-speed wireless Internet connections.

Kathleen Williams operated the eighteen-room Society Hill Government House in Baltimore. "Private baths and in-room telephones and TVs are essential if you're going to serve the corporate traveler," she told us. "Inn policies must be different, too. You must accept a variety of credit cards for payment, and check-in policies must be very flexible—business travel is canceled or changed frequently. And since business guests often travel by airplane, they arrive and check out at all hours of the day and night!" This, of course, affects an inn's staffing patterns.

Inns located in business destination cities may also have to provide conference rooms and meeting arrangements for their guests. The nine-room Loveland Inn in Loveland, Colorado, added a new meeting and reception center by purchasing another building across the street. The owners, Bob and Marilyn Wiltgen, renovated the new property with the sole purpose of adding space for executive sessions and banquets—for as many as sixty-six people.

Business travelers may be conscious of costs. Inns often have to meet or beat the room rates of downtown hotels and motels. Anne Hillestad, former innkeeper at the ten-room Queen Anne Inn, located four blocks from Denver's central business district, told us she did a lot of work with businesspeople. To stay competitive, they offered guests a corporate rate on Sunday through Thursday nights.

"Urban innkeepers need to be flexible," says Dick Jones, innkeeper with his wife, Mary, of Chelsea Station, a five-room, two-story brick Federal Colonial they opened in 1984 in Seattle. "We fill a variety of lodging needs for a diverse clientele with wide-ranging interests. Unlike travelers to other kinds of inns, our guests are not single-minded in their interests. Business guests mix freely with getaway couples and tourists visiting the many attractions Seattle has to offer."

Destination inns are those that are destinations in and of themselves. Locations that are "away from it all" have a magnetic pull for aspiring innkeepers—idyllic little spots out in the middle of nowhere with nothing but the beautiful countryside. Other destination inns may be beautiful old houses or mansions that beg to be turned into inns. That's what happened to Owen and Ripley with Boydville.

The problem with a destination inn is that people can sit still for only so long before they drive themselves—or you—nuts. Then they want to see or do something—shop, visit an attraction, swim, whatever. If your inn is a farm in the country, will it offer enough to keep them occupied? You do not want to be in the position of baby-sitting your guests. You want to be able to enjoy their company, and they yours, without overdoing it.

RULE 2: WRITE A BUSINESS PLAN
"The bed-and-breakfast business," says Murray Burns, innkeeper at the Eastlake Inn in Los Angeles, "needs the same sort of talents, the same sort of up-front analysis, the same sort of ongoing control systems that any viable, profit-making business needs."

Business plans need not be terribly elaborate, but the more detail you can put into them, the better. We have a general description of the business plan in chapter 4. You can also get one of the books that steps you through the process. Some aspects of inns, however, will require adjustments to the standard business plan and some details that you might not think of including. Some websites offer business plans specifically for inns, but exercise some caution before jumping into buying one of those.

Decide how formal you want your plan to be. You might be able to get by with something handwritten on the back of a napkin, but if you write a more formal plan, you will be treating innkeeping as a business from the beginning.

When Dennis and Cindy Marquis were negotiating to buy Maplewood Farm in Gardenville, Pennsylvania, they realized they would only have half of the down payment required and would have to look to friends and family for the rest. Says Dennis: "Based on our knowledge of having worked at an inn, and being computer-wise, we put together a seven-page business plan, complete with three-year revenue and cost projections. We tried to prove that the numbers worked, and that with our acquired innkeeper skills, we would be successful and thus able to pay back the bank plus the private investors."

RULE 3: RESEARCH

Peter Scherman of the B&B Team in Scottsville, Virginia, one of the leading inn brokers in the country, spends a lot of time with buyers trying to get them to understand what they can do: "I've always encouraged people to do more studies before they start, to look at one's financial objectives and try to assess case by case: What can I do in this location with the facility itself, and can I do it and get the rates I want? What are the things people are willing to pay for, and can I do them here? So many people go in with an expectation of doing something, but they don't coordinate the physical plan with their financial objectives. What can they do to what they've got in order to charge more? It's a dynamic kind of thing. You need to appraise the situation every few years as the market changes."

No single resource book you thumb through or website you browse will answer all your questions. The burden is on you to investigate and compile data from many primary sources.

Do some background work on the area you're interested in. If you have found a mansion you want to convert to a B&B, what is there in the area to sustain it? If there's a town you want to move to, does it have at least one of the previously mentioned magnets going for it? And more important, is the magnet known to the traveling public?

Even if there is an attraction like a factory outlet near you, will it attract the kind of guests you want? Owen and Ripley thought that Boydville's location two blocks from the Blue Ridge factory outlet center would guarantee traffic. They put hundreds of brochures in the center without stopping to think that many discount shoppers would have no interest in a high-end luxury inn. Shopping was, and remains, simply a neat thing to do for guests who are already coming for some other reason. Eventually the outlet center closed—so there's another thing to keep in mind: How permanent are the attractions around your proposed location?

Apply common sense to your research. Use the resources of your local chamber of commerce, which in the end will be a good contact for you. Most local chambers double as the visitors center for the area, and all now have more and more elaborate websites that will send considerable traffic your way. All chambers have good research on the potential of their areas. They'll also tell you what other inns operate in the area, so you can judge whether there is room for another.

Many states and regions also have publicly funded visitor councils or tourist promotion agencies. These groups have the same capabilities as a chamber of commerce but focus only on tourism. They may even operate a tourist information center; if so, you should certainly visit it. When you've opened your inn, you will find that you become a visitors center yourself, so you should look at what resources the operating ones offer.

Talk to the local or regional inn association, if there is one. Most regions with any concentration of inns will have an association, and it will give you good advice, possibly even telling you whether an inn is for sale in the area. If the association president tells you there's no more room, take it very seriously. At least realize that you will have to come up with some kind of niche that isn't being filled by any other inn. Many areas are so popular that they are now attracting a lot of illegal—that is, unlicensed—bed and breakfasts, which cuts into the business of those that follow the rules. If that's the case where you're thinking of buying, it would be wise to talk to the local planning and zoning department to find out what, if anything, is going to be done about this. You'll do everyone a favor if you at least put the bug in their ear that you are less interested in an area that allows unfair competition.

Visit other inns. Better, stay in them, and pay the full rate—never ask for a discount when you do this kind of research. Always tell the innkeeper that you are thinking of opening an inn in the area. Be honest about your intentions, and do not take too much of your host's time asking questions. The goodwill of other innkeepers is critical to your success; do not do anything to jeopardize that goodwill. When you say what you are doing, the other innkeeper may turn his or her back on you, but in our experience, this has been rare.

You should also talk to local bankers involved in the hospitality industry. Introduce yourself as a future small-business owner who may well seek financing. Interview the bankers, asking about their expertise in the lodging field in general, and inns in particular. Bankers may be conservative, but they have a wealth of financial data on business operations and the history of successes and failures in the area.

The yellow pages of the local phone book or an online version is also an invaluable resource. When the time comes to assemble your team—architect, builder, attorney, and so on—it will come in handy. Such a local business directory can also help you answer other questions during your research, such as whether there is a good Chinese restaurant near your new inn.

RULE 4: KNOW WHAT YOU ARE
Inns are the ultimate in niche marketing. Every kind of inn that could be created probably has a market somewhere. You need to make sure, however, that your niche is not so small that you can't survive in it. Finding those guests that want your kind of inn requires that you be able to define clearly what you are.

Spend considerable time—you'll do it for the pleasure anyway—writing down what sort of stage you're trying to set and what kind of experience you're trying to create. Although we often pride ourselves on the distinctiveness of our inns, the truth is that at least some people perceive a kind of sameness to them. Really, does every inn have to put a piece of chocolate on the pillow? It has become such a cliché that even the Sheraton does it now.

Some writers have taken to mocking the worst aspects of the "typical" inn. Cynthia Gorney, writing for the *Washington Post*, heaped scorn on the stereotype as long ago as 1987: "What we have here are seventeen-room Victorians furnished in the kind of chairs that history museums rope off with little gold braids. We have hand-polished silver brush and comb sets here, and sherry decanters made out of cut crystal, and leather-bound copies of *David Copperfield* for your reading pleasure. I ask you: You want to read *David Copperfield* on your vacation? You want to sign over your weekly paycheck so you can tiptoe around a bedroom full of spindly things that look like they're going to smash to smithereens if you're the type who can't see too well in the morning?"

Heed this. Avoid the stereotype. In order to be a success, you have to be idiosyncratic, maybe even eccentric. You have to be, above all, more than people expect. If at least one guest a week doesn't say that, or something like it, you're not sufficiently different. Carl says that innkeeping is a profession of chiefs, not Indians. He's absolutely right.

The inn is an extension of your personality. Memorable innkeepers are people of strong personality and conviction. Their inns are not for everyone, which means that there are going to be people who don't like it. But if you get rid of your personality, you might as well be a Marriott franchisee.

On the other hand (there's always another hand in this business), potential guests are often overwhelmed in areas where there are large numbers of inns. The amount of research they have to do to find the "fit" is getting to be an increasing problem in those areas. The end reaction is often, "They're all pretty much alike, anyway." Not true, but that means you have to think a lot more about what kind of website you create (more on this in chapter 6).

RULE 5: DO A TRIAL RUN

Rabbit Hill innkeeper Maureen Magee made the most elaborate effort we know of. For two years, she and John ran a B&B home-stay in their house. "We had two rooms in our own house. We lost all kinds of money because we converted the rooms, plus we were giving away dinners. We had predicted the losses. The object was to test what we had already said we were going to do." According to Maureen, it was the most important part of their ultimate success.

Working as an innkeeper for someone else, through an apprenticeship program, as an inn-sitter, or as a resident innkeeper, will help prepare you for the realities of inn owner-ship better than anything else. Dennis and Cynthia Marquis of Maplewood Farm did this to test the waters before diving in: "We learned what to do, as well as what not to do, while work-ing as resident innkeepers at the Wedgwood for over a year. We opened our own place and hit the ground running."

At the very least, be an observant guest at a number of inns. Certainly you'll copy details of one or another, but you'll never duplicate a great inn.

One final hint: Inn broker Peter Scherman told us of an inn in Virginia that set up its website a full year before opening. It was constantly updated with progress on the building, how the rooms were coming along, and so on. When it opened, it had a full house.

--- ◆ ---

4

About the Money

"THE BIGGEST MISTAKE THAT INNKEEPERS MAKE IS NOT
REALIZING HOW MUCH MONEY IT TAKES."
                                    —Jean Hendrick

When you think about owning your own inn, you probably create a bit of a fantasy, imagining just the building you want, with your own brochure, website, and signage, and with no preconceptions from a previous owner. It will be the perfect inn in the perfect place. It's a good idea to keep that vision in a safe place in your heart. It will be worth measuring the reality against it.

If you start from scratch, even in the best of circumstances, it will take time to get established. The good news is that the Internet makes this much easier and quicker. The bad news is that there's a lot more competition in desirable areas, so you're going to have to be taking a piece of business from others—hotels, motels, and other bed and breakfasts.

If you buy an established inn, on the other hand, you will have to pay extra for the going business and its goodwill, and you may not be aware of all the problems dogging the business when you take it over, such as a chef about to quit, a housekeeper who drinks, or a slate roof that needs replacing. In other words, there are drawbacks either way.

Of the approximately 25,000 inns in America, at any given date about 10 percent are officially for sale and an equal number are for sale for the right price. With such an inventory of going concerns, it is our firm advice that you are better off buying an existing inn than starting from scratch. Ripley and Owen, who have done three from startup, heartily endorse this. You may find that your occupancy rate drops on first taking it over— that's to be expected—but you will avoid so many other pitfalls that you'll thank your lucky stars you took this advice. You can buy and keep the inn as is, reposition it in the marketplace, or upgrade the room amenities. But the zoning and other needed governmental permits and licenses are already in place, and you can open the doors the day of the real estate settlement. *Caveat emptor,* though. We'll explain more later in this chapter about things to be on the lookout for when you buy an operating inn.

Nothing is sadder than watching nice people who put everything they have into an inn get slowly ground down by the harsh financial realities of inn ownership. We've known of several inns that opened in good times with high-interest-rate loans, assuming there would be all kinds of business. We've seen owners buy inns in high-priced markets, assuming all the figures given them by previous owners were true, only to find they'd been had. We've also seen owners in this position try to get out of ownership and still make a profit, and sometimes they have actually done that, leaving a later owner holding the bag.

None of this does any of us any good. It is in the best interest of all inn owners for all inns to succeed. It astonishes us to see people come into our towns, which are extremely popular for inns, and buy something without ever talking to another inn owner about what to expect. And many real estate brokers actually discourage them from doing so. But it's important to talk to and stay with other inn owners. Ask questions. And if you become an owner, be willing to help those who come after. It's just as important for you as it is for them.

If you do start from scratch, how do you get through those first few very tough years? Often one partner holds a job outside the inn. This becomes the base that keeps the whole operation from sinking. Innkeeping can be a tax shelter for this income. When you hit black ink and retire from the nine-to-five job, celebrate your freedom.

When you start your dream project, whether you are starting from scratch or buying a going operation, you should gather a team to help you. Your team may include the following:

• *CPA and lawyer.* Find those with commercial and lodging expertise, so that you and they do not have to reinvent the wheel. They will review the books of an operating inn, suggest the best form of ownership, and write a partnership agreement, if that is called for.

• *Architect, builder, or contractor.* You need someone knowledgeable in historic renovations or, if your inn is starting from scratch, in additions, alterations, and construction. He or she also will understand local zoning regulations and can tell you not only how your project should proceed, but whether it should proceed at all. We cannot stress enough how important it is to understand zoning laws, including those for historic buildings and districts. We have seen cases in which additions have had to be torn down because these regulations were ignored at the outset.

• *Real estate agent.* You want someone knowledgeable in commercial real estate, not just a part-timer in home sales. There are a growing number of agents who make a special practice of inn sales. Talk to some of their previous clients—preferably from a couple of years back—to find out if they were truly valuable partners.

• *Inn consultant.* He or she writes the business plan, with income and expense projections and the key assumptions behind them, such as occupancy rates and room charges. A good inn consultant is a kind of scout who works for you in unfamiliar territory. Sometimes this role can be taken on by a real estate agent, but in that case we usually recommend that you use a buyer's broker—a person you pay rather than one who is paid by the seller. Even in the best of cases, the seller's agent is going to have divided loyalties, and you need the best independent advice you can get.

You need to assess your own financial strength so that you can guide your team to the best solution for you. Buying or starting an inn is going to be a costly proposition, whichever way you go. So you have to give yourself the best possible chance of success. If you have the financial wherewithal to hold out for a while, then starting from scratch may work: You can build or renovate exactly what you want and where you want, and then build your business. If you don't, then buying (or leasing) an established inn is the wisest course. Of course, there's no guarantee that an established inn will support itself over the long haul, either. Careful financial management is always important, even with a strong business.

When Margaret Perry bought the Thomas Shepherd Inn in Shepherdstown, West Virginia, in 1989, the inn had been successful for five years, had a strong following and a good reputation, was in a college town and a recreational area, and was near national historic parks. But Margaret had to work very hard to make ends meet. The major reasons: a new, and higher, level of debt service and a reluctance on the new innkeeper's part to raise rates. Eventually she did raise rates and made a success of her tenure there.

As important as where your inn will be is how large it will be. On that decision will hinge all kinds of financial decisions: how much money you will need to cover operating costs, how much repairs will cost, how much your rates should be, how many employees you will need, and so on. Unfortunately, there is no simple answer to this question.

"How much house can you afford?" is a charming real estate phrase that just doesn't apply in this situation. You don't really know how much you can afford without figuring your costs per room and potential income per room. That's another good reason to look at buying an operating inn: At least you have some idea of what the property can gross.

One good hedge is to consider how expandable the property is. Is there enough land to add on? Can you do it appropriately for the style of house? Are there other buildings nearby that offer expansion possibilities? Will there be zoning issues if you want to expand?

There are other considerations besides size. Private baths are no longer an option, but a necessity. How luxurious the bathroom will be is the question all potential guests are asking.

Double whirlpool tubs are our number-one sought-after in-room amenity across all our market segments at both the Wedgwood Inn and the Biltmore Village Inn, and every innkeeper we know says the same thing. The next most requested item is a fireplace, then a king-size bed. The question of how upscale you want to be is not a slam dunk. In this new century, guests are asking for luxury but less willing to pay for it. That's certainly a squeeze for the aspiring innkeeper, and it will make a lot of difference in the value of the property you might want to buy.

THE FINANCIAL NITTY-GRITTY

Create a spreadsheet for every property you want to consider seriously. One section should be your *basic cost of the assets,* the amount you will pay for such things as the property, furnishings, website, and closing costs. This is essentially the final sale price. For starters, use the asking price for your figures, though you probably will negotiate a lower one. Into this section also go your planned improvements. Break these down as much as you can. Get good renovation estimates from your area, and then add some extra money. We always think it's going to cost less and take less time than it really does.

You need a section on *operating costs,* which include your travel, research, legal costs, telephone, inspection, and appraisal. An inspection of the property by a contractor or home inspector is essential, since he can find problems that you would not see by yourself. Do not take the owner's word for this. Most may be honest, but people have different ways of doing and looking at things. What may be at best a minor nuisance to me might be a major problem to you. Identifying those weaknesses will help you bargain on the price.

When you are thinking about buying a property, keep in mind that there are limits to what you can ask from a current owner in the way of inspections before a contract is signed. At some point, he or she is going to get irritated by the constant coming and going, and you'll have to show that you are serious. It is usually the practice to offer a letter of intent when you get serious about a property. It doesn't obligate you to anything, but it lays out your expectations, and an owner will feel more confident about giving you financial information—or possibly saying that he or she is not interested in proceeding on those terms.

The usual inspection areas include water, septic, radon, insect damage, environmental, structural, and mechanical. Even with the results of these inspections in hand, your worksheets are truly going to be estimates. Everyone will advise you to estimate high, since even in the best of situations you will miss something. As Jean Hendrick of Pilgrim's Inn on Deer Isle, Maine (now owned by Rob and Cathy DeGennaro), told us in 1992, "In this 200-year-old building, there are things breaking even as we speak!"

Another section is *working capital,* that chunk of money equal to at least three months of operating expenses that smooths out the times when your anticipated cash flow turns into a trickle.

You then need to figure *operating costs:* utilities, advertising, insurance, supplies, food, ongoing repairs, outside services, telephone, Internet, amenities, replacement of linens, and so on. Calculate these in one-month intervals, and recognize that they won't be constant from month to month. Dues for your association memberships are annual, for example, as are property taxes. In fact, since you are probably going to pay more for your property than the previous owner, your property taxes will increase, perhaps substantially. That is one good reason to put more of the purchase price into goodwill; furniture, fixtures, and equipment; and marketing materials than you might have intended, since that will at least reduce the property tax you will have to pay. If you are going to be operating for just seven months a year, some costs will be negligible for parts of the year—but then, so will income!

Now you need to calculate projected *income.* These figures should also be in one-month intervals, with attention paid to the seasons. Most inns have high and low seasons (connected by "shoulder" seasons), and weekly cycles within each month. Identifying the patterns will help you allocate resources for those times when you need extra. Putting operating costs together with projected income will tell you when your *greatest exposure* will be—that is, when you will have the most cash dipped out of your money well. That tells you how much you need to have as a reserve.

Room income is a perishable commodity—much more perishable than a piece of fruit. Like an airline, you are selling a seat. Once the plane is gone or the night is gone, your chance of selling is gone too. In the lodging business, rooms have a substantial gross profit margin. However, the inn's fixed costs (debt service, insurance, and taxes) are high. Much like a hospital, an inn is expensive to operate whether or not the beds are occupied.

But the good news is that the actual cost of selling a room is quite low, often 10 to 20 percent of income. The marginal additional cost of filling that empty room includes laundry, chamberperson, amenities, food, supplies, and a minimum utility cost.

Consider this example: Say you have a ten-room inn with an average rate of $100 per room. Your average expenses are $7,000 per month, and your average monthly income is $7,000. You have 300 potential room-nights in a thirty-day month, so your occupancy rate is 23 percent. What is the additional cost to book your seventy-first room? Your expenses are fixed at a little over $20 per room, whether it is rented or not. You can see then that renting a suite at $150, a standard room with a private bath at $100, or a shared bath at $60 will all cost you the same. But the income from the most expensive room is far greater than that from the least expensive. You work slightly harder, and your fixed costs remain the same.

You have two choices as to what to do at this point: You can lower the rate to book those extra rooms, as many inns do in their slow season, or you may decide to hold out for the higher rate, since the margin is better. The more rooms you have, though, the more likely that they will be filled at the lower rate and give you a larger income. And at least in recent years, guests have been on a bargain binge, looking for all the amenities for the price of a motel room. You should not bet everything on current conditions, though; even from month to month, you'll find guests changing. In 2004, the bargain hunters were dominant in the first half of the year; later in the year, the luxury customers were back, booking the high-priced rooms. Setting rates is not easy, and we have devoted a section to it in chapter 5.

HOW BIG?

You no doubt have realized by now that there is no easy answer to the size question as it relates to profitability. If you have four rooms, maintain no staff, own the house with no mortgage, and your occupancy rate is 30 percent on an average room rate of $175, you will have a very nice profit margin indeed.

That's not how the standard business model works, though. You're expected to invest 20 to 30 percent and show an annual rate of return of 15 to 20 percent.

Most innkeepers are going to have a substantial debt to service in the form of a mortgage. If you really are starting from scratch and have a sizable mortgage, 30 percent occupancy and $125 average room rate may have you slowly sliding toward bankruptcy. You can quickly see that with a hefty mortgage, the top amount you could realize is limited, even at an impossible (and undesirable) 100 percent occupancy rate.

New innkeepers typically overestimate their potential income. The standard occupancy rate for a mature inn is 30 to 50 percent (5 percent higher in a village or urban setting), and it has been in that range for more than a decade. This may be disappointing to you. Aspiring innkeepers typically assume they will be booking at a minimum of 50 percent when they start out. Occupancy rates are meaningless except as a measure of unused capacity. As Kathy Hemes, former owner of the Albemarle Inn in Asheville, North Carolina, is fond of saying, "It's not the occupancy rate that's important; it's the bottom line."

Our discussions with innkeepers have turned up a strong sense of what size is required to be profitable. It is hard to make money on an inn of fewer than eight rooms if you have any sub-

stantial mortgage and your occupancy rate is less than 40 percent at a low to average room rate. A smaller inn must be taken
on with great care. You'll need to spend more time than you
think making sure that you have a good location with high
occupancy potential, and you'll need to leave yourself plenty of
working capital.

Carl found that the original six-room Wedgwood wasn't big
enough to satisfy the demand that it had in large part created for
itself. In 1991, he and Dinie increased the number of rooms to
eighteen in three separate buildings. Although the operation
now creates more headaches, at least they have more cash flow
to work with. One other major advantage, Carl says, is that the
inn actually became easier to run as it got larger, because they
were able to hire innkeeping staff in addition to housekeepers.

Carl and Dinie expanded the inn in 2000 to add more function space and to add four suites with whirlpool baths. They
also upscaled other rooms at the Wedgwood. Their newest,
most expensive suites book up first, adding profit to their bottom line. Ripley and Owen are looking to expand their current
six rooms to eight or even twelve. Bigger pretty much is better,
at least in our estimation, as long as you can keep the essential
personal touch that makes an inn what it is. The goal is to reach
an economy of scale that meets your needs as owner-innkeeper.

The community in which it is located often imposes limits
on the size of an inn. Asheville, for example, limits inns to eight
rooms maximum in a residential neighborhood, and many other
towns have similar, or even more restrictive, limits. Durham,
North Carolina, for example, limits the size to four rooms. Size
limits will also affect your start-up decision.

The problem with growing is that you can lose touch with
the personality of the true B&B. This may be the hardest part of
innkeeping: getting the size (and price) right so that you can
keep up the property, have a reasonable life, and keep the personality that brought you into innkeeping in the first place.

Rabbit Hill's former innkeeper Maureen Magee told us that
she felt that eighteen rooms was the maximum she could manage and still maintain the personal contact with guests that

made her inn special. A high-energy innkeeping couple, she and John had twenty-one rooms, and if they said the inn lost its personal touch at nineteen, then it's clear that very few people would be able to manage more.

HOW MUCH INCOME?

There are two ways to look at value in your inn. One is your *equity,* which is the combination of the price you paid, improvements you have made, and the increasing value of your property. Equity usually is not liquid and is useful to you only for use as collateral for a loan or when you want to cash out.

For a working inn, equity is irrelevant to your operations. Gross profit and cash flow are what count. Your *gross profit* is the money you have after expenses and before taxes and depreciation. Your profit is what enables you to operate, in addition to the working capital that you set aside to get you through the early years and times of slow cash flow. If you ever have to dip into the inn's equity for operating income, you should be nervous about its profitability.

Figuring your tax deduction, including depreciation (a job for accountants), gives you your *pretax profit.* Then, after you pay those taxes, whatever is left over is *net profit.* Given the ways inns work, any positive net profit is good (some people say this is true of any business), and even negative net profit isn't all bad; as long as it doesn't go on too long or get too high, it can shelter the salary you pay yourself.

You have to accept that you aren't going to make a lot of money in this business, but you can have a good life on a very small income because so many of your expenses as owner and manager can be covered by the inn. According to Kit Riley Cassingham, a Denver real estate agent, consultant, and former innkeeper: "The profit in inn ownership really comes when you sell it. Few innkeepers become millionaires by operating an inn, but many accrue riches of another sort. Those who do find innkeeping a lucrative business say that profits depend on how much time and energy is invested. Though a majority of innkeepers do not become wealthy, we can live a rich and rewarding lifestyle. Living with your life partner like royalty in your dream house, in your dream destination city, far removed from the hassle of commuting and the stresses of city life—the grass is greener at the inn."

BUYING AN ESTABLISHED BUSINESS

If you buy an established inn, much of the work has been done for you. You'll pay more for it, but you should get quite a bit in return. You may encounter considerable difficulties in evaluating a going proposition, however. Be prepared to have the following questions answered by the current owners, real estate agents, tax agencies, accountants, other innkeepers, or other sources of information:

• What is the annual percentage of occupancy? Is it in line with other, similar inns in the area? If not, why not? Also check with an independent source to verify that percentage.

• Does the amount the business is taking in seem reasonable? You might think that an odd question, but sellers want to make things look good. Look at the average occupancy rate for the area to determine the probable average occupancy rate for the inn; you can do the math fairly accurately.

• Will you be able to retain current guests? As the number of inns increases, repeat business is dropping. Inn guests like the idea of being able to try different inns and don't mind telling you that they are doing so. That's innkeeping life.

• Is the property up to code and current in its licenses? Are they transferable to a new owner? If not, will they be difficult to obtain?

• What zoning restrictions are on the property? Will local zoning permit expansion? Is there room to expand if you want to?

• How do the neighbors feel about the inn? Will they be good neighbors for your guests?

• Does the business owe any back taxes? You don't want a huge liability hanging over your head.

• Does the owner say that more is taken in than shows on the books? This surprisingly common assertion, besides being dishonest and illegal, makes an accurate income projection impossible. If you find yourself taking such an assertion seriously, you are letting your desire for a particular property override your good sense.

• Is there evidence of deferred maintenance (routine maintenance not done on systems prone to fail without it)?

• Is the business involved in any legal actions, such as liability suits or claims for nonpayment? Are there any mechanics liens (work done by carpenters, etc., that has not been paid)?

You and your accountant eventually need to see the financial records. If you are a serious buyer and have been properly qualified by your agent, this shouldn't be a problem. Look at three years' worth of records. The books you see probably won't have been audited, and you may not be able to evaluate them. This is when you should ask for help from your accountant; he or she will ask questions about the figures that may not occur to you. Beware of any handwritten books that look as though they were done all at once—we have seen this. Usually this means they *were* done all at once and therefore bear no actual relationship to the business. Electronic books, of course, won't reveal this, though time stamping does help. Use logic when dealing with the numbers: If something looks too good to be true, it usually is.

Also ask to see a couple years of federal and state tax returns relating to the business—either corporate or personal ones, depending on the form of organization of the business. You won't get to see these until you've signed a contract, but a proper contract allows you to withdraw if the returns do not show what they have been represented as showing.

In your contract, be quite specific about what is included in the sale price. The owner should give you a listing of equipment, furnishings, and so on. You will have to replace anything that is taken out or not included. It can cost $3,000 to $4,000 to buy and outfit a bed—and that is being frugal. Also make sure you have an accounting of, and get credit for, any outstanding room deposits, gift certificates, or other obligations.

When purchasing an established inn, you also need to allow for a transition and renovation period, and figure out what to do with the staff, if any. Unless you believe the business has been

run in a slipshod way, you will probably do best to keep whatever employees currently work there, even if you change their
duties. In fact, sometimes the staff is one of the best things you
can get with a going operation. Good inn workers are hard to
find.

GO FIGURE

For the sake of comparison, here is a set of figures for three different purchasing possibilities.

	Cozy Corners 6-room Going inn	Prosperity Hill 12-room Going inn	Scratch Inn 8-room From scratch
Price	$800,000	$1,600,000	$450,000
Costs			
Down payment	160,000	320,000	90,000
Closing costs	30,000	50,000	15,000
Inventory	10,000	20,000	15,000
Other costs			
Moving	20,000	20,000	20,000
Deposits	3,000	6,000	6,000
Rent, living	0	0	9,000
Approvals	0	0	12,000
Renovations	10,000	20,000	300,000
Furnishings, equipment (added)	15,000	30,000	150,000
Total cost of assets	$248,000	$466,000	$617,000
Working capital	60,000	100,000	80,000
Total cash needs (first year, less mortgage)	$308,000	$566,000	$697,000
Revenue projections			
Year 1	$110,000	$225,000	$50,000
Year 2	121,000	245,000	80,000
Year 3	135,000	270,000	110,000

One thing worth remembering here is that Scratch Inn costs
more up front but will have a lower mortgage, which evens
things a bit—assuming the owner has that much cash up front.
Otherwise, the cost of renovations will be part of the mortgage,

which puts Scratch Inn on the same footing as the others, but with less revenue at the start. Because of the Internet, starting from scratch isn't as scary as it was ten years ago, except that the competition is so intense now that you might not meet your revenue projections unless you can offer something extraordinary.

In all cases, the plain fact is that *economies of scale* give you a greater return. This means that when you are doing things on a large enough scale that the initial fixed costs are spread over a larger base, this lowers the cost per unit and increases the profit per unit. Hard figures put together by the Professional Association of Innkeepers International (PAII) bear this out. According to its 1989 survey of the bed-and-breakfast industry—and the facts have not changed in the intervening years—the larger the size, the greater the return: "Smaller (two- to four-room) properties do not make money. With six to seven rooms, the owner-innkeeper starts making a profit. An inn with 11 to 20 rooms is averaging an 8.23 percent return on initial investment including owner time (excludes property appreciation). With more than twenty rooms, owners see a 28.7 percent return." You may not like to think of things in such terms if you just want to create a romantic retreat, but it's a lot easier to create romance when you have the resources.

Inn broker Peter Scherman offers a useful way of evaluating an inn you're thinking of buying as a business. Although the owners of a small B&B may think of it as a business and run it that way, the marketplace may not recognize it as a business because it does not affect the value of the property. So the owners may not really be selling a business, but simply real estate. This is not placing a value judgment on whether it's good or not; it's only saying that the marketplace will pay for what a property is—not for what someone wants it to be.

"As its size and revenues grow, the value of an inn grows, but it's only at the point that the value of the cash flow and the ability to support debt service exceed the value of the assets being sold that it really qualifies as a business. If the cash flow can support 70 percent debt service plus operating expenses and still have money left over, the inn is a business.

"If you are looking to buy an inn, you need to understand what you want and how to meet your objectives. Are you looking for a return on investment, a lifestyle, or a happy medium between the two? It's important to understand what your objectives are. But often a buyer's objectives don't meet his or her financial capabilities." To ensure that they do, it's helpful to write a business plan.

WRITING A BUSINESS PLAN

Writing a business plan for your inn serves many purposes. People often think a business plan is necessary only if they need to raise money from investors or banks. But even if you are relying on your own resources, it helps to have an outline of what you thought you were going to do when you started so that you can check your progress. And if you have an active partner, it is a formal statement about how money gets spent, on what schedule, and what is expected from the expenditures.

You won't be able to complete your business plan until you have selected your property, but you can work at it from various angles as you narrow your search. As you work on your plan, you will discover that you do it in pieces, not from beginning to end. You'll work first with the numbers that are known quantities, such as how much you can spend and what some of your fixed costs are. Other numbers will require some research. That research will lead you to a descriptive section of the plan, before bringing you back to the numbers.

A business plan form has become reasonably conventional. The basic parts of a plan and what should go into each are as follows.

Executive Summary

Every plan begins with a summary. You write it last, when you have a plan to summarize, and then you put it first. It describes your hopes and dreams and objectives in plain, direct language. Writing down your dreams sheds some light on them, so don't be surprised if this part causes a bit of pain.

Think of yourself as a banker when you write and read this part of your plan. If in a few pages you cannot convince the skeptic in you that your plan will work, it probably won't. One of the reasons to write it last is so that you won't be tempted to manipulate the numbers in your plan to justify your summary.

The executive summary begins with an introductory paragraph or two explaining the ambience you are trying to create and what kind of paying guests you expect to attract. It should capture your excitement about your inn.

Several paragraphs summarizing each section of the plan follow the introduction. Include enough financial detail to give a good sense of the viability of the project. Executive summaries are often written as expanded tables of contents; use that form if it suits you.

Description of Purpose

In a brief section a page or so long, describe your proposed inn, or what you propose to do with your going inn; what clientele you want to serve; and what your business goals are.

Here is where you distinguish yourself from other inns in your area. What are you going to offer that sets you apart from them? Or, if it makes sense because of the amount of business in that area, how will being similar work to your advantage?

Show how your inn fills a need in the marketplace. Don't just rely on generalizations; place your own inn in context.

Detailed Description of Inn

Put here all the detail you can about what sort of atmosphere you want to create and how you will cater to your guests. You will come back to this section of your plan later to see what is appropriate in terms of design and to remind yourself of what you said you would do. If you can state your ideas clearly and then flesh them out with convincing details, you will be able to carry others along with your vision. If you cannot, you've discovered a weak spot in your new enterprise.

This part can be useful for two partners, who may suddenly discover as they go through the exercise that they have differing views. One may want to put candles all through the inn, whereas the other thinks that is expensive, dangerous, and tiresome. Putting details on paper brings up these disagreements early on and allows you to work them out, preferable to having an argument in the middle of the dust of renovation. These written details also will be helpful when you are creating your brochure and website.

You can work on these two descriptive sections before you look at many properties. Keep in mind, though, that you may not find the perfect property that allows you to carry out your exact plans. If you plan to do a mountain aerie with rustic appointments catering to an outdoor crowd, you know to avoid certain kinds of buildings. But you may run into the perfect Victorian in a village at the foot of the mountains and fall in love with it. Then you'll have to rethink everything.

Creating your "perfect" inn is an organic process that evolves with experience and changes over time. The nonnegotiable points in your model will become clear, as well as the areas that are flexible. Let your ideas evolve as you refine them.

Marketing Plan
Your marketing plan is essential, especially if you are starting from scratch. You cannot simply open an inn and expect that your market will walk up to you. Well, it probably won't, but the Internet has changed everything. (Much more about that in chapter 6.) If you buy an existing inn, your marketing plan will focus on increasing business, reaching out to new clientele. Your plan has two parts: market research and selling activities.

Market research and analysis prove to you and your potential investors that you do have a market. This is something else that is made easier when you buy an existing inn. The former owners can fill you in on most of this and may even have a written marketing plan that they will share with you. You certainly should make that part of the transitional training that you write into the contract.

Although travel is big business, only a small part of the traveling public goes to inns, and it divides further according to the type of inn. Budget-conscious travelers will go for homestays; affluent professionals, business owners, and executives are drawn to upscale B&Bs or country inns. You need to know whether the kind of people you want to appeal to will want to come to your inn.

Do some informal research among the kind of people you want to reach. Talk to travel editors and other innkeepers. Stand outside the tourist information centers in the area in which you intend to buy and ask questions; dress nicely and carry a clipboard on which to take notes. Visit with travel professionals in the area; you'll find them at the chamber of commerce, visitors center, regional tourist bureaus, and inn associations. If there are no such resources or other hospitality properties in the area, be wary: you may be considering the wrong location.

After you are convinced that you have a market in your preferred area, focus on how you sell your rooms. These will include some advertising, but advertising in the traditional mode usually is not effective for the small or medium-size inn. Putting an ad in the local newspaper draws almost no business (travelers looking here are usually price conscious and shop down the column, looking for the best bargains), magazines (with some exceptions) very little, and radio and television almost none. And these are very expensive outlets. A quarter-page full-color ad in a regional travel magazine can cost you as much as $15,000 and get you only five guests. By the next month, you're forgotten.

A major change in the last decade is the Internet. It's so important that there is a discussion devoted to it in chapter 6, along with other methods to get your inn noticed. Adapt those ideas for your inn, and put in your business plan the ones you are going to use. Your marketing budget will be very limited for the job it has to do, so you must take great care to spend wisely.

Operations

Under this heading go the details of how you will get your inn going and keep it running. This should be the easiest part of your plan. It should address these issues:

• How you will undertake renovation, and how long it will take.

• When you plan to start marketing, and with what expenditures.

• Where you will get labor, either full-time or contract.

• How you will deal with licensing and zoning, if they aren't part of your purchase.

In this section, you are supporting your requirements for capital and proving that you have estimated accurately. Inns, like all new or expanding businesses, often founder on this issue. *The single most common cause of new business failure is running out of money—working capital.*

Management Plan and Organization

Management issues are tied to how you are organized. The bigger the company and the more formal the organization, the more people you need to operate it. A simple sole proprietorship makes you the owner and manager. A full-scale corporation requires officers and a board of directors.

In the management section of your business plan, explain your choice of organization. Lay out the role each owner will take. Introduce key people who may not be owners but will be important to the inn. For each person mentioned, include a brief résumé in the supporting material at the end of your business plan.

Sole proprietorship. The sole proprietorship is the simplest form of organization. You own everything, it's all reported on your personal income tax return (with some additional forms, of course), and you get any profit you make from your venture.

The disadvantage of the sole proprietorship is that you are liable for all losses. If you go bankrupt, your creditors can go after you for everything you have (within reason), as determined by the bankruptcy court. If you lose a liability suit, all your personal estate is at risk.

This is an issue of considerable importance to innkeepers, who usually have everything they own tied up in their businesses. If you lose such a suit, you really do lose everything. So a sole proprietorship, though simple to operate, does expose you to more potential risk. Most American businesses have chosen this form.

Partnership. A partnership is more complicated than the sole proprietorship, but not much. You should draw up a partnership agreement and take care of all the issues of who owns how much equity, how you bring the venture to an end should that be necessary, and how to handle the withdrawal or death of one of the partners. In a partnership, the partners have full liability, with the same disadvantages as a sole proprietorship.

In *limited partnerships,* the general partner bears most of the liability and is the active manager. Other partners are limited in liability. This form is often attractive to prospective inn owners who need help coming up with the necessary capital. Such limited partnerships can be unstable, because the general partner has to spend time demonstrating to the limited partners that their money is being properly handled. Buying out limited partners early is usually a good idea.

Inns are almost always partnerships, in fact, though they often do not have that structure. If you choose this form, you should write a partnership agreement that spells out all the difficulties you can anticipate. Like a business plan, it can anticipate and eliminate by previous agreement most of the unpleasantness resulting from major breakdowns in communication. It can ensure that the business will survive a disagreement or the death or disability of one of the partners.

Corporation. There are two types of corporations: the regular (C) corporation and the subchapter-S (S) corporation.

Incorporation is the most complex type of legal organization. It is good for large-scale operations with complicated products or services and a need to operate with stability over a long period. If a company is expected to have a long life, it will need to be able to change owners (shareholders) relatively easily without affecting the business.

A corporation has to register with the state of its incorporation, make sure it has annual board meetings, keep a stock and record book, file regular reports, and pay extra taxes for the privilege of this type of organization. It also pays income taxes *before* distributing any dividends to the stockholders (trying the tempers of those who see this as double taxation of dividends).

Because of these various complications, there are not many corporations compared with the other kinds of organizations. Why, you ask, would you choose this form? For innkeepers, the corporate form of organization would seem to be an unnecessary complication of life.

There are several reasons. First, if you sell the business, you have a ready estimate of its value: the stock price you have set, plus its physical assets. You can raise money quickly through the sale of stock should you wish to do so. Most important, the corporation itself, not the individual stockholder, is the legal entity that bears liability. If there is a lawsuit based on a liability claim, it is the corporation that is sued and the corporation's assets that are at risk. Your personal assets are not owned by the corporation and thus are not in danger in such a suit.

Fortunately, most inn-goers have not gone in for this kind of suit, nor are inns known to have the deep pockets that makes such suits worth pursuing. But minor suits have been popping up more recently, with a resulting steep increase in insurance rates. It may be that in coming years, more innkeepers will incorporate and possibly will be encouraged (or required) to do so by lenders and insurance companies.

Another good reason for corporate organization is that it requires greater care in accounting and reporting. As a result, corporations are not audited by the IRS as often as other businesses. Still, corporate organization might not seem to be worth the trouble for innkeepers, except for the interesting subcategory the S-corporation.

In exchange for certain limitations, which are no problem for this type of business, S-corporations are allowed the protections of the corporation yet can still have direct pass-through of profits and losses to the stockholders without double taxation. Boydville was an S-corporation, as is the Wedgwood, so we're both advocates of this form.

Limited liability company. A relatively new form of organization is known as the limited liability company (LLC). Most states have passed legislation allowing this form of organization. It allows the liability protection of the corporation and the simpler registration, reporting, and taxation requirements of the partnership. The LLC may be an ideal form of organization for the small inn. Biltmore Village Inn is an LLC, which was required by the Small Business Administration in return for a low-interest loan guarantee.

Financials

If you are out to raise money, this is the part of your plan that bankers or investors will eye the most carefully. Write your chart of accounts on a spreadsheet, or use a computer program to make calculating and recalculating easier. Even if you are financing the whole business yourself or are writing a plan to guide future growth, creating a financial plan will give you a way to gauge your expenditures as you start up or renovate and expand your inn.

Include in your financial plan all the kinds of revenues and expenses you can imagine.

Your income should include the following:

Room sales
Restaurant meals
Sales of gifts and books
Receptions and meetings

Expenses include such things as the following:

Salaries (especially your own)
Benefits (health insurance and retirement plans if you can afford them)
Rent (if you lease your building from the corporation, for example)
Cost of food
Cost of goods sold (books, mugs, T-shirts)
Furniture and fixtures
Accounting services
Outside services (subcontracted services such as inn-sitting)
Auto expense

  Advertising and printing
  Legal fees
  Licenses
  Office costs
  Remodeling
  Maintenance and repairs
  Utilities
  Taxes
  Supplies
  Telephone
  Internet access and cable TV
  Cost of new or redesigned website
  Insurance (liability, fire, and theft)
  Dues, subscriptions, memberships

Do a summary projection for five years. It should be more detailed at the beginning and brief at the end (monthly for the first three years and annually after that, for example). Use the projection to show anticipated profit.

The care with which you've done the earlier part of the plan will show here. If you have been filling in the numbers for each step, you will now begin to see the results.

These numbers will be your guide to operation. Once you start up or are growing your newly acquired business, refer to them often, comparing your actual performance to your plan. If there's a discrepancy, do something to fix it or determine why there's a gap between your projection and the actual numbers. You cannot predict a hurricane, but if one happens, you need to make adjustments to your projections and use them to figure out a way to get back on track.

Your numbers should reflect reality. Try not to be too enthusiastic in your projections. We have suggested the return on investment you might expect for various sizes of inns. At the very least, you want to be operating in the black after five years; the IRS takes a dim view of operations that lose money over long periods of time.

Profit percentages are typically slim—it's a rare inn that shows a margin of 25 percent—so projecting high amounts is unrealistic. If you expect a margin of 4 percent, in order to show a profit of $8,000, you might have to have sales of $200,000. Some of the expenses of running an inn will astonish you. The suggested chart of accounts from PAII has a separate line for towels and linens—not an expense line you are likely to find in most businesses. Dane Wells of the Queen Victoria Inn in Cape May, New Jersey, told us, "We estimate that to keep this building attractive to the marketplace and in good condition takes between $20,000 and $40,000 of capital expenditures each year"—and that was in 1992. Of that, $2,000 alone was for linens. Painting the building cost $15,000 to $20,000.

The constant maintenance of any building can be surprisingly high, and historic buildings are exponentially higher. When Owen and Ripley redid Biltmore Village Inn, they replaced all the plumbing, the electrical system, the roof, and the heating and cooling systems, and they repainted the whole thing, inside and out. But maintenance started the first year, and—like many innkeepers—they usually paint a quarter of the interior and exterior each year. You can end up replacing locks, doors, windows, washers and dryers, refrigerators, freezers, stoves, and whirlpool pumps, not to mention upgrading furnishings, draperies, carpeting, tile, and on and on. Don't underestimate this aspect of innkeeping.

There is another category of expenses that does not go into the monthly analysis: capital improvements. These expenses are significant, but they are not treated by the IRS in the same way as ongoing expenses; they have to be spread over a period of several years, and the number changes according to the type of improvement. For the purpose of working out your monthly analysis, you can ignore these. When it comes time to file your taxes, have your accountant help you with the capital improvement expenses and depreciation calculations.

A word about depreciation: You can depreciate anything that is part of the business. This can save you a ton on taxes, which is very useful at the beginning of your innkeeping career. However, if you sell before your property is completely depreciated, you will have to do what is known as "recapturing" depreciation. The short explanation is that you'll have to pay the government a chunk of money for depreciation you took. For that reason, you may not want to include every square inch of your building as depreciable income-producing property. Talk to your accountant about how you want to do this. If you're expecting to be in business less than seven years, it's a very big issue. One recent change in the code allows you to expense certain kinds of equipment that you used to be required to depreciate—a good thing.

Your spreadsheets provide detail, but you also need a summary of the figures to make your plan complete. The earlier comparison of the three inns shows one kind of summary; there are other methods as well. However you arrange the figures, the summary has to contain all the totals under general categories. Your financial summary will be the basis of most of your discussions with bankers and potential investors.

RAISING THE MONEY

Now you have all this stuff written down, but you still don't have the money. How have all these other innkeepers—thousands of them—managed to do it? Here are some ways to raise the money, and there are certainly others:

• Sell your home and put your equity into the inn. This is the most common method.

• Cash in assets you and your partner have managed to accumulate, such as savings, investments, 401K plans, or retirement plans that can be used this way.

• Keep one partner working outside the inn. The job income qualifies you to borrow from a bank, credit union, life insurance, or the Small Business Administration.

• Attract investors to a limited partnership.

• Look into state economic development funds, which may provide low-interest guaranteed loans. Check with your state commerce department or county or city economic development corporation. You'd be surprised how accommodating some of these folks can be.

make choices about where you will spend your money. There is never enough money to do all you want.

The first thing potential guests see is either the inn itself or your website or brochure. (More about brochures and websites in chapter 6). So your inn has to have "curb appeal." If your tastes tend toward the formal, use traditional signage and formal gardens. If you love flowers, plant them everywhere. If you like the country theme, have a plow or old wagon as part of your sign. Some people might find this hokey, but you're not looking for them as your guests. You're looking for people who like what you like.

Don't falsely advertise in your brochure and website, and don't promise more than you can deliver. Don't overspend on the facade to the detriment of the interior. Every innkeeper can tell you stories passed on by guests who were drawn by the outside of a place that looked fabulous, only to find the interior disappointing. Guests have told us of an inn out west that attempts to be a version of Tara (an odd thing for the desert anyway). It has pillars that don't quite reach to the portico and fan windows with dividers but no glass. Anyone who knows the real thing can spot a fake at once and will never be a returning guest.

Seacrest Manor, an eight-room B&B opened in Rockport, Maine, in 1973 by Leighton T. Saville and Dwight B. MacCormack Jr., was named 1988 Inn of the Year by the readers of Pamela Lanier's guidebook. Leighton, who unfortunately died of cancer in 2001, attributed much of their success to a philosophy of honesty: "Be honest in how you portray your inn, and deliver on your promises." Dwight continues to operate Seacrest successfully.

If you want to open a historic inn, you don't have to spend a lot of money for an authentic look. Be careful about displaying too many valuable pieces. Accidents do happen, and although theft is rare in the inn business, you don't want to be the one who proves the exception. You also want to avoid creating an oppressive museumlike atmosphere.

Most historic inns are either Victorian or red-brick Colonial, as these are the styles that were built when the country was in its glory days. A Colonial building projects more formality than the Victorian, so creating the right mood and making your guests feel comfortable may require a bit more effort on your part. Victorians have a lot of odd little nooks, which make decorating a delight. In general, most innkeepers look for an older building on the assumption that most guests want to "step back in time." And some towns will not allow a new building to be made into a bed-and-breakfast inn.

If you love one of these styles, by all means go for it. Familiarity can be an advantage, as your guests will have an idea of what to expect. But on the other hand, familiarity sometimes can be a disadvantage. People can get tired of seeing the same old thing. Inn-goers are an odd collection of the loyal and the fickle, which is why it is so important for your style to be your own—something you love and are comfortable with, not something you copied.

When Victorian goes wrong, it tends to slide into the fussy and overly cute. Some people can be put off when innkeepers go overboard with bed furnishings: too many pillows, too many coverlets, too many flounces, flourishes, furbelows, and froufrou. But other guests simply love all that.

There are some cases where historic inns would be inappropriate. In an outdoor recreational area serving hikers, rafters, and skiers, a sturdier style of inn is preferable. The rustic inn will always be popular, and many mountain inns go back to the late nineteenth and early twentieth centuries. If this is the kind of area that attracts you, you're probably the kind of person who prefers that style anyway. In this kind of setting, especially if you want to serve families, you certainly don't want fragile antiques around.

In 1990, Arna and Jeff Fay opened the Fox Creek Bed & Breakfast in Fox, Alaska, an old mining town about ten miles north of Fairbanks. It's a rustic inn, but Arna emphasizes that the inn has all the amenities, including two whirlpool baths. The inn is Arna's full-time job; Jeff is a freelance photographer. B&Bs have become very popular in Alaska, and Jeff and Arna believe they are selling their lifestyle and personalities as well as lodgings. Both were born and raised in Alaska, and they attempt to present the inn as authentic Alaskan.

The historic and rustic styles tend to dominate because most inns are still in New England, the mid-Atlantic states, and California. As more parts of the country develop inns, other styles should leaven the mix.

Then there's the eclectic, a term often used to be complimentary about a mishmash of no particular distinction. But it can refer to a charming expression of an innkeeper's personality. Hillbrook Inn is such a place. Gretchen Carroll created a country inn from a Normandy farmhouse built around a seventeenth-century log house. The whole thing spills down a beautiful hillside. Inside is a mix of pieces Gretchen has collected from all over the world. Turkish samovars and Russian paintings sit side by side with contemporary American pieces. Entirely distinctive yet harmonious as a whole, Hillbrook is a perfect expression of its owner's tastes. It enchants its visitors because it is so unlike anything else they would find.

Today the trend is toward more informal surroundings. Owen and Ripley chose a much more formal style for Boydville and less formal for the Inn on Montford and Biltmore Village Inn. It seems that people are becoming more interested in being comfortable than in high style.

Given this trend, be careful not to make your historic inn too formal. Conversely, if you have an informal inn, exercise some care to show that you aren't just throwing your place together willy-nilly.

Jean Hendrick keeps Pilgrim's Inn rustic, but she's also quite sure of how she wants things done: "We are not going to make any compromises because we're informal. I'm not going to dress up in a long skirt with a little bow, because that's not me. Whatever our backgrounds, good points, and faults are, the inn is also that." In other words, good fresh food, comfortable rooms, cordial hosts, and no faded tablecloths will have guests coming back.

YOUR STYLE

You cannot be all things to all people. Your strength comes from your originality and your ability to fill your niche. Not everyone is going to like your place—not everyone has to. One of the major mistakes that new innkeepers make is to bend their presentations to what they think the caller wants. New innkeepers also fall into imitation. True originality can be scary. If it has never been done before and is not expected in your area, will it catch on? Can you survive until you find your proper guests?

Susan Schwemm, former associate editor of *America's Wonderful Little Hotels and Inns,* says that in her many travels looking at inns, she has noticed how certain regions have particular kinds of inns. "Inns all tend to be similar in certain regions," she says, "even to the point of serving the same kinds of breakfast." There is, it would seem, safety in numbers.

This is not an unreasonable assumption: Guests in a certain area are more or less trained to expect certain things. New innkeepers will not go too far afield for fear of disappointing guests' assumptions. Nevertheless, you can meet many expectations and still make a virtue of difference. It seems to us that prospective innkeepers move into an area and get captured by the regional style before they develop confidence in their own. Most of us take quite a while before we're able to convey the real flavor of ourselves and our inns. You would do well to travel to different regions of the country to try out inns and ask questions. You should be stimulated in ways you don't expect and more encouraged about your own originality.

An area like Cape May proves the exception to our rule about striving for uniqueness. Cape May has built its reputation as a town of Victorians. Being different here probably wouldn't be a good idea. By joining together, the town and its inn owners have created an ambience for everyone. This has the effect of making your inn seem to be a branch of a larger enterprise. You may not like that; if not, don't go to an area that is identified strongly with a particular style.

The possibilities for developing your own niche are endless. A number of inns, for example, are Christian in orientation. This can work quite well if you make your focus clear. Bill and Helen Goodbrod run Ye Olde Library Bed & Breakfast in Jersey Shore, Pennsylvania, as a Christian B&B. As it happens, there is

not much to do in their area, and the house is neither histori-
cally important nor filled with antiques. But because they've
identified their strengths and played them up, it does well for
them.

Bill and Lola Coons used their interest in nature to create
Down to Earth Lifestyles B&B—as unusual an idea for an inn
as you can imagine. Located near Kansas City, the house is
"earth-integrated," and the approach carries through everything
they do. In an age of environmental awareness, this comfortable
house with eighty-six acres and an indoor pool has to make
people interested. Lola and Bill opened in 1982 and tell guests
that they are "midwestern through and through," from their
architecture to their style, decor, and food.

With natural and healthful foods so popular today, another
idea might be to cook with fresh ingredients from the inn's own
garden.

Why Style Is Important

Establishing your style is not just a matter of whim; it is essential to your ability to compete. You have to go beyond imitation of what is already out there if you want people to come to
your inn.

When a veteran observer like Cynthia La Ferle, who was one
of the industry's opinion makers in the 1980s and early 1990s,
said she was tired of the same old thing, you can bet this attitude showed up in her writing. If you can't get written about
because you're perceived as just another imitation operation in
a crowded market, then you lose the important advantage of
editorial endorsement. This has become even more true in the
new century. So many inns today seem to be doing or saying the
same thing that they have a hard time establishing their unique
value.

If, on the other hand, you can establish your own special
ambience and style, you'll attract writers, often quickly. Your
object is to be one of a kind, no matter how many other inns
are out there. Most likely you will create a new inn audience for
your area by doing so, and if you increase—and satisfy—a new

group of travelers (*and* all the people they will tell), you'll do some good for yourself and the other inn owners around you.

Bobbi Zane, publisher of a newsletter for new and aspiring innkeepers, *The Yellow Brick Road,* advises every inn owner to create a mission statement—a one-paragraph description of who you are and what you do. The paragraph could even be shortened to a single phrase, like a slogan, and used on all your marketing pieces. This exercise not only will help you focus on what makes your inn unique, but also will benefit your marketing efforts.

Maintaining your own style doesn't mean ignoring everything else. Keep up with what is going on after you open your inn. Innkeepers get notoriously out of touch as they spend more and more time in their own inns and see less of others. Standards change, and you need to accept these changes without giving up what makes your inn special.

BACK TO THE FINANCIALS

Once you have established how you want to do your inn, there is a ticklish financial issue left: You need to be able to project your income. If you have done your research with some care, you should have some idea of occupancy rates for your area. With a good place for a sign, key distribution points for your brochure, a great website that is marketed appropriately, and excellent relations with surrounding inns and hotels, you may be able to figure on getting 40 to 50 percent of the prevailing occupancy rate for your area when you open. You will almost certainly be disappointed by how low the actual figure is.

Be as conservative as you can in your calculations. It is not at all unusual for a new inn to have an occupancy rate of just 10 percent its first year and build rather slowly from there. Although you should expect an increase of 10 percent a year at first, you might have more or less, depending on how quickly your inn catches on, how aggressively you market it, and how low you are at the start. The Internet has made an enormous difference in how fast an inn can get off the ground. One inn that had a well-designed website up and running well before the inn itself was ready had a high occupancy rate from the start, because potential guests were already anticipating going.

Your occupancy may well be seasonal. If you are in New England, you are likely to be closed for three to six months of the year. With a season only six months long, you cannot have more than a 50 percent rate, even if every room is filled every day you are open. If you are a weekend place, as many inns near large cities are, then you may have a rate of 28 percent—and count yourself lucky for that.

So unless you are absolutely sure and have plenty of evidence to back you up, don't figure your occupancy rate high. You need an accurate rate in order to establish your pricing structure. If you have no idea what your rate will be, figure 10 percent. If you have less than that, you won't really have much of a business anyway, and at least you'll know that you can support your investment.

Deciding What to Charge

Pricing is one of the most ticklish questions in innkeeping, yet we have seldom seen it discussed. On your room rate depends all your chance of success: Without income, you have no business, and without adequate income, you lose your business.

Pricing is a delicate balancing act of what you want (or need) to charge and what the traffic will bear. If you set a rate that will give you a comfortable income from the beginning, you may be priced out of the market. You cannot charge $175 for a room in an average rustic inn where the rate of similar inns is $100. If area inns are so crowded that you could rent a hammock on your porch with no bathroom privileges, then you might get that rate for a time—or after everyone else is filled. But we wouldn't want to have to deal with your guests. And we wouldn't make a bet on repeat business or word-of-mouth referrals. Some areas of the country, such as Oregon, have low rates in general. An inn that could charge $250 in Newport, Rhode Island, would get $175 at best in Seaside, Oregon.

One of the maxims of the hotel business is that every $1,000 spent building a room should translate into $1 in the room rate.

If we equated all the costs for Scratch Inn with room costs, we would get a rate of $41.50 per room. Of course, that would be quite cheap. Such rates would certainly compete with the economy hotels and motels, but the economics are quite different for motels, and that rate would doom Scratch Inn.

Many inns market themselves as being upscale or even luxury accommodations. Yet one of the problems of pricing is the old notion that because of the term B&B and its European associations, we're cheap alternatives to hotels. You'll hear innkeepers complain about this perception often.

Claudia Tzucanow of Brunswick Manor in Brunswick, Georgia, told us: "We have noticed that many of our inquiries are from people who are hunting for bargains. They have the mistaken impression that B&Bs are cheap places to stay. When this is obvious, Harry politely suggests that they consider a motel." That has not changed since the first edition of the book. If anything, there is even more emphasis on bargain hunting. Endless stories and websites have led the public to expect that there are incredible last-minute bargains out there—and sometimes there are. The end result has been later and later booking. It used to be that you would book your rooms a month ahead; now a day ahead is not unusual. This adds considerably to the anxiety of innkeeping.

Part of this is a result of a commoditization of the business in the traveler's mind. The airlines and cruise lines were the first down this road. The end result: bankruptcy for some, or consolidation in the hands of a few carriers who can manage the economies of scale. This is not possible in the inn business, and we fear that we are going to see a shakeout down the road.

Hotel chains made what we consider a major mistake in the recession of the early 1990s: They began an advertising binge to tell customers how cheap they are. According to one marketing consultant, "Such advertising tells the customer to pick hotels just on price. It destroys brand loyalty and turns hotels into a commodity."

Our business, even where we offer lower rates, must avoid becoming a commodity. We cannot afford—any of us—to advertise enough to survive as a commodity. And most inns don't want to compete that way. But the hotel chains have not held still; even midlevel motels now offer breakfast, high-speed Internet connections, whirlpool tubs, and on and on. And at higher prices than they used to.

A rich tradition of bargaining in other parts of the world has never gotten established in America (with the exception of car purchases), and pricing has always been a take-it-or-leave-it thing here. But we are getting more and more guests who bargain, especially businesspeople looking for a place for meetings. Frankly, we dislike it; bargaining is most certainly not what we got into the inn business to do.

So to establish what the market will bear, you have to look at other prices. Cast a large net—all lodging establishments within a ten-mile radius. If you have a more sparsely populated area, then widen your circle. You will soon find that there is a range for your area.

Sometimes the pricing constraints will make it impossible for you to operate your new inn successfully. This happens when either there are not enough guests to support a new inn or the other inns in the area are so long-established that their fixed costs are relatively low, and they can realize a reasonable profit at much lower room rates than you could ever charge. This is a difficult situation for a new inn, and it means you aren't likely to get established without being prepared to go a number of years carrying financial losses. You may not be in a position to do that.

The easy answer to establishing a price is the traditional business one: add together the total dollar amount of your annual expenses and your desired annual return on your investment, then divide that figure by the anticipated number of rooms rented. For example, for Scratch Inn you might have annual expenses of about $45,000 after start-up (we're being conservative, and we're not including much of a salary for the innkeepers). Figure on a generous rate of return of $10,000 per year, for a total of $55,000. With an occupancy rate of 15 percent, or about 350 rooms booked, this formula would say you should charge an average of $157 per room. If you have different rates for different rooms, as inns usually do, you're looking at a range of rates from about $110 to $200.

The new inn suffers from a double whammy. It has higher acquisition costs and, consequently, mortgages than other inns in the area. And at the same time, other inns have an established clientele and a built-up business. That clientele expects a certain rate in the area; if that rate is $140 a night, you may well be able to get a high rate. If, however, the going rate is $85 a night (and this is more common), you're going to have a hard time persuading the cost-conscious traveler to give you a try.

So now what? You could reduce your costs and the rate of return you are willing to take, at least at first. Suppose you take no return (not uncommon), and you figure you'll close down in cold months to save on utilities and upkeep. You might be able to get the total down to $40,000 a year. That would give you an average of $115 per room, with a range of $85 to $150.

On the surface, that seems to be doable, and things might get better as your occupancy rate went up. Yes and no. You're still putting your lowest rate at the average for the area. So if price is the major consideration, your least expensive room will not be booked until everyone else is half full. Under these circumstances, you probably won't make your projected occupancy rate, and you'll end up farther behind.

In many areas, there is a psychological barrier at $150 (and another at $200) for double occupancy. Many travelers will balk at that point because they simply do not think that a B&B, particularly one in a rural area, should cost that much. Many innkeepers who have prices above $150 end up referring a lot of guests to other inns that are "more affordable."

After the $150 benchmark some innkeepers go to per-person rates. For example, $65 per person works out to $130 per room, double occupancy. That sounds better to the customer. The drawback, of course, is when you have a single traveler. Most inns drop the rate for a single traveler back from the double occupancy rate: $130 double would be $110 single, for example. That's a lot more than $65, which you would have to honor if you offer per-person rates. The way around this is "$65 per person, double occupancy."

Inns priced in that higher range are often used as benchmarks by others in the area, who, by pricing $5 to $10 below, pick up the traveler who does not think there will be any difference in quality for that difference in price. This is one way for a new inn to get started, if the lead inn in the area doesn't feel threatened and is willing to refer people on.

Pricing strategies don't just follow the numbers, though. They are often an outgrowth of the innkeeper's style just as any other aspect of the inn is. You have to be able to quote your rates, believe in them, and make them stick. If you don't believe that your inn merits the rate you're charging, you'll start reducing it before you even hear what the customer has to say. Then where will you be?

Jean Hendrick, despite her already high occupancy rate, excellent restaurant, and stellar reputation, deliberately set the rates of Pilgrim's Inn below those of other inns on Deer Island. Another innkeeper, Charles Hillestad of the Queen Anne Inn in Denver, set his prices by watching closely what the local luxury hotels charged and then pricing lower. Such a policy ensures that the occupancy rate remains high, assuming that there are guests to be had. You might call this a predatory pricing policy, and in some cases it works. But it isn't usually something a new inn can manage, especially as the inn market matures. Jean has been in business for twenty years and does not have a huge mortgage. She and her husband, Dud, have amortized a large part of their investment already and can easily afford to defend their turf with lower prices. But inns that start with rates that are too low may have a hard time bringing them up to the right level.

Pricing experts will tell you that trying to compete on price indicates naïveté on the part of the owner who tries it. Established inns, if they wish to be competitive, can reset rates low enough to beat back your challenge. Competing on price also means you are not paying attention to what you should be doing: offering a unique inn experience. You must differentiate yourself from the others by some means other than price. If and when you are well established and are perhaps threatened by newer inns (if our business ever gets so predatory), only then might you want to start competing on price.

There is good news, however, from Gretchen Carroll of Hillbrook Inn, whose rates are quite high: "I was told by a friend who had successfully started an inn that I should charge a much higher rate than anyone else in the area. She said that people would pay the rate and actually think if it was that expensive, it had to be good!" Gretchen's place *is* good, so people have reason to think it's worth the price.

Owen and Ripley have had a similar experience at Biltmore Village Inn. One guest who took a room at full rate in January 2004 believed that all the other inns' rates were so low that "they couldn't possibly be as good."

You have now entered the interesting area of guest psychology. Pricing doesn't just depend on where your rates are in relation to the competition. Your prices also tell people what you are and what they are to expect. If you are competing on price, then you have to give a greater value per dollar than your competitors. If you are competing on the uniqueness of the experience you offer, then you need to convince potential guests that your price is an expression of how valuable this unique experience is.

A useful exercise in setting rates is to look at the amenities you offer and what guests would be willing to pay for them. Start with the average rate for a clean double room with private bath at a local motel. To that, add something for the fact that you offer much more service, something for your breakfast, something for your comfortable sitting rooms. Then add on for whirlpool tubs (add a lot for double whirlpools), for fireplaces if you have them, for king-size beds, for views, and so on. You might be astonished to see how high your rate should be for what you offer. If all innkeepers were confident in what they offer, we might well see the end of all the jockeying over rates.

The only way to know whether your guests will buy this is to try it. Inns still depend on word of mouth and repeat business. Guests won't return if the price is out of line with the perceived value, and they certainly won't recommend you to others. Self-deception can cause a great deal of misery for the new innkeeper. You believe your inn is unique and exceptional, you set prices and advertise accordingly, yet you have no repeat business. That tells you something, and you need to listen to what it's telling you.

In general, inn-goers in the past have been more quality-conscious than cost-conscious. But the market is expanding, and new guests in the twenty-first century are paying more attention to price. And unfortunately, the percentage of repeat guests is going down, especially in areas where there are many competing inns, as people like to try new inns as a different experience.

The old conventional wisdom among innkeepers was that the most expensive rooms booked first. Later, the most expensive and least expensive booked first. Now the conventional wisdom is that people are looking for value rather than luxury. Price is not the only indicator for them; they might well take the middle-priced room first. You have to do something to indicate that the value is worth the price, whatever that price is. That occasionally requires you to do some real selling.

One last thing to consider is the need to change your rates from time to time. In highly seasonal areas, many inns customarily charge seasonally adjusted rates. Some Cape May inns have five different rates within a twelve-month period. And most innkeepers review and often change their rates annually. According to Leighton Saville of Seacrest Manor, it's important to keep up with inflation, but don't raise your rates so high as to price out your repeat clientele. You might offer your repeat guests the old rate for a period, in order to give them something special and encourage them to come back.

The best time to raise rates is just before the beginning of your busy season. Your customers are less likely to be sensitive to rate changes then. But plan ahead. One time, after a two-year period of not raising rates, Owen and Ripley decided to do so but forgot to tell people who were reserving for the busy season. As a consequence, they had half the month of October—the high season—at the old rates, and they had to be very careful not to quote the wrong rates to the wrong people.

MARKETING PLAN

Chapter 6 looks at the specifics for marketing your inn, but here we're going to get you thinking about marketing in general. The best way to ensure that your new inn has a fighting chance is to make sure you know ahead of time how you're going to sell it to customers. The marketability of your inn is tied directly to its design and execution. Working up a marketing plan is a good way to focus on what you're really trying to do: sell an experience.

Why do you need a plan? Because without it, you are likely to use your limited resources wastefully. Marketing is very expensive. It can take 5 to 15 percent of your gross revenues; the newer the business, the higher the percentage. This can be a big bite out of your new inn's income.

Most innkeepers follow some version of Carl and Dinie's three-point approach to marketing the Wedgwood: 1) minimize paid advertisements (innkeepers don't have a lot of money to spend); 2) maximize guest referrals and repeat business; and 3) maximize professional referrals, free search engine exposure, and free publicity from the media.

The Wedgwood's marketing plan has worked wonderfully for them. Here is the basic outline. Carl calls it SOS, for *situation, objectives,* and *strategy.* It has worked for many new innkeepers.

1. Analyze your *situation.* Look at the following:
   - history and goals of the inn.
   - available investment.
   - occupancy and profit potential.
   - external market segment and size.
   - market trends.
2. State your *objectives.* They might be one or two (but probably not all) of the following:
   - increasing occupancy, market, profit share, or return on investment.
   - improving image and reputation.

3. Set out your *strategy,* including package, price, promotion, and publicity, using whatever means are available:
   - personal selling and advertising copy.
   - media outlets (both print and online).
   - financing.

Try your first pass on the back of an envelope. Summarize in one sentence how you see your situation. Do the same with your objectives. Then jot down a rough strategy.

Here's an example:

Situation: Scratch Inn has good weekend business, but midweek occupancy is very low.

Objective: To increase occupancy on Monday, Tuesday, and Wednesday nights by 25 percent over the next twelve months.

Strategy: Develop a marketing plan to attract new clientele who have the flexibility to travel midweek, such as dentists, hairdressers, retirees, and business travelers. Try to reach them by using the following methods: advertising in specialty media outlets; offering credit for referrals from professionals; developing a special midweek package; offering lower midweek rates; creating a print or online direct-mail sales piece.

Notice a few important details about this rough marketing plan: It is very specific about each step. It includes a narrowly focused problem, a precise quantifiable goal, and specific steps to reach it.

Further analysis of your situation may show that you cannot afford both the direct-mail piece and the advertising at the same time. Put them in preferred order, using affordability and expected return as criteria.

In order to complete the plan, you need to know what the possibilities are. Are you just blowing smoke, or are there actually some reasons for dentists to come to your town in midweek? You need to do market research to find out.

Market research simply means getting information that will strengthen your decisions and give you a solid basis for your expectations. You can ignore the facts, but do so with your eyes open. For example, because of an emotional attachment, you might decide to locate your inn in an area ten hours from any major population area, where the occupancy rate is low, and where your rates also will be low. If you're set on doing this, you should know up front what problems you'll face.

Your objectives are the key. It is important to make these goals specific in order to pursue them efficiently and coordinate them with the rest of your operations.

The following guidelines will help you set good objectives:

- Keep them quantified and clear.
- Make them measurable so that you can gauge your progress.
- Have several objectives so that if you miss one, you may accomplish others.
- Specify time frames, such as by month or season, short-term (one to two years), or long-term (three to six years).
- Set them high enough to be challenging, yet low enough to be realistic.
- Make a simple list or chart of your four or five key objectives.
- Set all objectives with an eye on affordability.

DEALING WITH REGULATIONS AND ZONING

As you begin the process of opening your inn, you're going to have to deal with the laws governing your operation. Inn owners have gained a reputation for skirting the law. One reason is that the laws get more complicated all the time, and we're often too busy to pay attention. You can ease this situation by setting up in a town that has experience in permitting inns or buying an existing operation.

With an existing inn, the permitting process should already be done. Many inns operate under zoning exceptions or special exemptions to certain regulations (historic buildings, for example, are often given alternatives to full compliance with fire and building codes). If you're buying an existing inn, you need to make sure that all those exceptions transfer. If they don't, you'll have to arrange for renewal or compliance before you take over (or have some assurance that this can be handled quickly and reasonably).

The major permits you need are zoning, fire, and health. Of those, zoning comes first and is regulated by the smallest jurisdiction that applies to you—city, township, or county. A quick visit to the city hall or county courthouse will get you early answers and will begin your acquaintance with officials who may have frequent contact with you as your business gets going. They also should be able to point you in the direction of the other two permitting authorities.

Fire regulations are usually handled by the county fire marshal or a local representative of the state fire marshal, sometimes by the town's fire chief. In many cases, there are exceptions to the rules if you have a historic building, your inn has fewer than four rooms, or it is two stories or smaller.

State-passed health regulations are almost invariably administered by the county. Food preparation is the most carefully watched. Many states do not allow B&B establishments to serve full breakfasts. If you do not want to install a commercial kitchen just to serve breakfast but are not satisfied with a simple continental offering, make sure that the state will allow you to prepare breakfast in an ordinary kitchen. Otherwise you may be faced with installing a commercial kitchen—an expensive proposition, especially in a historic house.

Both new and existing inns may face some serious problems as the federal government increases its regulations. New legislation in the areas of environment, health, and disability may cause hardship for some inns. Although most of these laws have exceptions for small businesses (those with fewer than twenty-five employees, in most cases), those exceptions may not last forever. And whereas with local laws there is a tendency to "grandfather" existing operations, federal and state law usually gives existing businesses only a certain amount of slack before requiring compliance.

The law that may affect us most is the Americans with Disabilities Act. This law does not provide exceptions for small businesses opening after 1993. Even established inns should consider what is going to be required of establishments with five rooms or more: a disabled parking space for every twenty-five spaces or fewer; elevators for three stories or more; ramp access for public areas where level changes more than one-half inch; 5 percent of rooms available for wheelchairs; 5 percent of rooms equipped for visually or hearing impaired (this requires such things as braille signs and flashing lights instead of alarms for fire).

The law does offer some concessions. There are exceptions for historic buildings, if the alterations would change the character in a serious way. Regulators are constrained to be "reasonable" in applying the requirements to existing buildings, and regulation should not inflict "undue financial hardship" on the business. Alas, there is wide area for disagreement here.

There probably will be no exceptions for new construction, although this rarely applies in our business, but the building code changes annually. The latest change in the international building code—the basis for all local codes—now requires new inn structures to meet commercial code. These code requirements are far more expensive than residential requirements.

6

Getting Your Inn Noticed: The Importance of Marketing

"THE SECRET TO SUCCESS IN BUSINESS IS TO FIND A NEED
AND FILL IT."

—Bernard Baruch

"GIVE THE CUSTOMERS WHAT THEY WANT."

—Marshall Field

Marketing begins with a concept. In innkeeping, that concept arises when you recognize a prospective guest's wants and begin to plan actions to satisfy them. Designing your inn was your first step in marketing.

A multifaceted marketing approach is needed, balancing the Internet with print advertising and business-to-business referrals. Your role as innkeeper, the human touch in this equation, also is crucial in earning repeat business and word-of-mouth referrals. Ultimately, your success as an innkeeper depends on all of the above.

No matter the medium, truth in advertising rules. Listing your inn's location as being in a popular destination city when you are really twelve miles out in the country is as bad as using a distorted fish-eye lens to photograph your smallest room for your print brochure or rack card. You'd better be able to back up all the sizzle with a steak—that is, a memorable, high-quality stay at your inn.

Many Internet guides promote discounting, rate reductions, and other such giveaways that copy the hotel-motel industry— which makes your inn just another commodity. In the long run, this may drive down room rates, attract more bargain hunters, and turn off the more traditional market segments of people looking for an inn experience.

MARKETING WITH YOUR INNKEEPING

Despite all you will hear or read, people choose an inn over a hotel or motel for one major reason: the experience. And the determining factor of the experience is the innkeeper. Innkeeping is intensely personal, and an inn is the extension of the innkeepers' personalities.

We believe firmly that the innkeeper makes the inn. If you offer every amenity imaginable, if your furnishings are priceless antiques, if you have staff available to cater to every guest's whim, if your views are stunning and your location without peer, but you are an absentee landlord, you will probably do well. But you will have set a magnificent stage without a play; an inn without the innkeeper's presence is only a shadow of what it could be.

Market your inn with your innkeeping. You're not selling soap.

People who go to inns, especially devoted returnees, say a major reason they return is the innkeeper and the individual attention he or she gives them. Travel writer Bernice Chesler called it "the *I* in innkeeping." Guests expect to be greeted by the innkeepers and spend time with them.

Innkeeper presence is the key to a pleasant inn, yet in some guidebooks it is passed over with a simple "friendly innkeepers." Newspapers, magazines, and websites often don't know how to deal with the innkeeper. It's as though cordiality and hospitality are so obviously a given that there is no need to mention them. Although some West Coast inns seem to thrive without a strong innkeeper presence, this is definitely not the norm throughout Canada or other parts of the United States.

One good reason to market your inn with innkeeping is to help dispel the mistaken notion that inns are simply cheap alternatives to motels and hotels. If you're going to charge guests three times as much as the nearest economy motel, you had better provide them with an experience that justifies the price.

MARKETING VIA THE INTERNET

Every innkeeper will tell you that the biggest thing to happen to this industry in the last decade is the Internet. It has changed everything about marketing.

The good news is that the Internet and the World Wide Web have made it much easier to get noticed—and to get a business off the ground. Owen and Ripley began Biltmore Village Inn in the Internet era, and the advantages have been clear. They believe it cut years off the start-up. Marketing is not any cheaper, but it starts to work much more quickly. Google AdWords and Overture are two pay-for-placement resources that can really jump-start traffic to a new or newly written website right away.

The Internet has practically replaced guidebooks. The reasons are fairly obvious: no space limitations, the widest possible distribution, instant updates. In effect, you own your own guidebook and can put in it whatever you want.

There are books about the use of the Web and how to create websites, as well as very fine website designers. Our purpose is not to tell you how to do all that, but to suggest the best ways to make use of this fabulous resource.

Web Estate

Your name becomes extremely important, because you are going to get the URL (universal resource locator) or web address that most closely matches that name. It used to be, and still is true to some extent, that inns would try to get to the top of the alpha-

bet, so that in any list you'd be the first to come up. That has
gone to an extreme, with inns' names now preceded with the
date the building was built: 1855 Queen Anne Inn, 1812 Zee-
landia House, and so on.

This ploy works for straight lists, but many tourism sites are
now moving to database-driven listings. What that means is
that the visitor picks out what aspects are important, and the
site sorts through its listings, presenting only those that match
the traveler's requirements. If the traveler checks *urban, AAA-
rated, king beds, Victorian* and you are missing any one of
those, you're not going to show up in the results.

Your web address identifies you when guests try to find you
using one of the search engines. Alphabetization is far less
important than what your name conveys. Searchers look for
something that identifies the area and often combine that with
"bed and breakfast" or "inn" in the search. If you can, choose a
name that is likely to come up on such searches.

Ripley and Owen feel very fortunate that the name Biltmore
Village Inn comes up high on the search results of a huge number of tourists coming to their area to visit the Biltmore House.
Not everyone can be so lucky. But if you haven't yet named
your inn, or if you think there's an advantage in renaming, by
all means consider what your name can do when it comes to
Internet real estate. Carl and Dinie own the URL new-hope-
inn.com (Wedgwood Inn is located in New Hope), and this
points to their inn's website, WedgwoodInn.com. Like Ripley,
they have taken advantage of the high-profile name of their geo-
graphic location to drive traffic to their website.

More than ever, your name is your location.

Search Engines

More gnashing of teeth and rending of garments are expended
on coming up high on search results than on any other aspect of
current inn marketing. Whole companies are devoted to
improving search engine results, and they can be expensive.
(There also is a *lot* of fraud in this area, so be very careful.)

The search engines give certain kinds of weight to different aspects of your website, so how you write it and name it are quite important. They try to reward well-written sites with a lot of information and many connections to other relevant sites. So how do you do this?

Your webmaster or designer will make the first pass (unless you're sophisticated enough with HTML to do your own site, in which case you don't need the advice we're giving here). But you have to give him or her the necessary information. The less specific you are, the more it will cost you in time and revisions to get it right.

We're going to go into writing and design in the next section. But one term you should get to know is *keywords.* Keywords are short, descriptive phrases like your slogan. They shouldn't be too long and are not complete sentences. Shorter ones are easier to work into text, but it's hard to get unique short ones. You can study how others do it by opening your browser, clicking on "view" and then "source," and voila! You can see all the keywords. To do well with the search engines, follow these rules (although they may change frequently, given the light-speed evolution of the Internet):

• Use significant keywords in the meta tag section of your website. You need to think about the terms that accurately describe your inn, its area, and what they both offer. Your name also goes here and carries a lot of weight.

• Come up with a different title tag for each page of your site, and make them accurate descriptions of the page content. This is what shows up when the search engines list the name of the page (or the site, if it is your home page). Certainly it's the name of your inn, but it can be longer.

• In the text, use your keywords several times, but not in an awkward or ridiculous way. Some sites have long lists of every word that could possibly apply to their area, but such lists can get you blacklisted by the search engines, besides looking ridiculous to the reader, so it can be a risky strategy. A version of this is hidden keywords—words that are the same color as the background so that they can't be seen. Search engines will punish a website they discover doing this.

- Use some headlines (headings), because the search engines like them and give them more importance than plain text. It also might help you organize what you want to say.
- Put your keywords early in your text, as the search engines usually put more weight there.
- Search out and cultivate mutual links to other sites. The best ones for inns are the established guide sites, associations, and state visitor travel sites. But there are all kinds of linking possibilities out there, and the more relevant two-way links you have, the higher your ranking is likely to be.
- Buying keywords (pay-per-click) is a bidding thing and can eat up money at an alarming rate. If you want to do this, make sure the amount you'll pay per keyword isn't so large that you'll use up hundreds of dollars for a small number of click-throughs.

There are many other techniques, and many more will certainly show up. It's unlikely that you'll be able to keep up with them all (and still run your inn), so get a good webmaster.

Website Design
We are big believers in making the fullest use of your website. You may be a small inn, but there's no reason why your website has to be small. Biltmore Village Inn has a website that is upward of forty pages and will probably grow (www.biltmore villageinn.com). In addition to the home page, it also includes descriptions of Asheville, reviews of restaurants, an events calendar, pictures and descriptions of all the rooms, a photo album, history of the house, all the past newsletters, an availability link, policy page, packages, guest comments, even Ripley's cookbook! The reason? Search engines like websites with plenty of relevant pages, and it's also possible to provide a lot of links from those pages to other relevant websites.

Ripley maintains the website himself, but the original design was done by a professional. You can maintain yours if you wish, but it can be time-consuming, so most innkeepers do not. If you maintain it yourself, you're able to make many more changes and improvements, but you're in trouble if something beyond your skills goes wrong.

When you set out to design (or redesign, because sites need to be renewed every few years), you need to keep control of the process. Start with an amount that you think you can afford to spend, say $1,500 to $3,000. What are you going to need to get started?

• Good photography. That means *professional* photography. Nothing looks worse in a brochure or on a website than cheesy pictures. Badly lit snapshots just do not work. You can throw in a few of your own pictures, but not for the outside view of the inn or for the rooms.

• Good graphics, if you want to use them. A well-designed logo adds a lot of zip to a site, but it isn't essential.

• Well-written text.

• A color scheme. The Internet is a visual medium, and colors are a kind of language with a certain impact.

Decide at the outset what you want to emphasize—which photos will be used on your home page, what kind of menu you want (side? top?), the kind of typeface you like (suggestions from your designer will help), and how much and what kind of text you want. You should write your own text, and we have lots of advice on that later in this chapter.

It's a good idea to look at a lot of websites from areas other than your own. Designers usually have plenty of examples of their work. We like Acorn Internet Services (www.acorn-is.com), partly because they are former innkeepers. Another fine outfit is Blizzard Internet Marketing (www.blizzardinternet.com). But there are many more, including many local to you. Purchase the very best web designer you can afford.

You can use an example you like to guide a designer, or leave it up to him or her. The more control you feel comfortable exercising, the more likely you'll get a site you like with the least (expensive) back-and-forth. Ripley worked with a Blizzard designer, basically buying as many pages as he could on a page-per-hour arrangement. There are as many such arrangements as there are companies.

Online Marketing Help

Following here is a list of recommended national online bed-and-breakfast inn guides. Besides inn listings for the guests, most also offer innkeepers chat rooms, resource directories, and other content geared for both the aspiring and the seasoned innkeeper. In order to determine what is right for your inn in your location, you'll need to make your own comparison of rates and services of these guides; they often offer various levels of service within each online guide, too. This list changes as often as does the Internet:

Bbonline.com

BedandBreakfast.com

BnBinns and iloveinns.com (print guidebooks published by American Historic Inns)

LanierBB.com and travelguides.com (print guidebooks published by Lanier Publishing)

Theinnkeeper.com

Virtualcities.com

In addition, it is critically important to be listed on special-interest, local, regional, and statewide websites and search engines. Most guests search by geography first, especially in well-known destinations. For example, a Google or Yahoo search may begin, "Canada, Ontario, Niagara Falls, bed-and-breakfast inns" People often misspell searches, so factor that into your keywords, using "Niagra" as well as "Niagara," for example.

No one can afford to be in all these online guides and maintain a presence in the print media too. Nor could you possibly use so many guides to the full extent possible and still keep your content and availability up-to-date. Visit each website, and research how many unique visitors click through to your state and region. Then make an informed decision on which websites you'd like to try. Often they'll offer (or agree to) a free three-month trial. Ask.

In summary, Internet marketing is multitiered. According to Trent Blizzard, founder of Blizzard Internet marketing, "A healthy website typically receives traffic from a combination of free search engines, PPC search engines, lodging guides, destination guides, and niche resources." And savvy innkeepers also have e-newsletters, promotions, and special rates offered only online.

Here are some other online resources for innkeepers-to-be:

Professional Association of Innkeepers (paii.org)

Yellow Brick Road Newsletter for Aspiring Innkeepers (yellowbrickroadnl.com)

BnB Magazine (bnbmagazine.com)

The B&B and Country Inn MarketPlace (innmarketing.com)

This book's website: www.bbstartrun.com

Your local and state associations (try your city, county, or state name, followed by .gov, .com, or .org)

Google or Yahoo searches on the subject area of your choice, such as "Canada, British Columbia, inns for sale" or "USA, Oregon, Portland, seminars for aspiring innkeepers"

OTHER MARKETING OPTIONS

Other avenues to explore as you search for ways to market your inn include public relations, promotions, publicity, and paid marketing.

Public Relations

Public relations is work you do to get attention without paying for it. This includes such things as personal visits to area businesses, successful placement of stories in the media (particularly travel publications and websites), speaking and teaching engagements, and doing interviews as an innkeeping "expert." Some of these things may come to you accidentally, but on the whole, you do have to work for them.

Travel writers, particularly, do not do a lot of digging for new inns to write about. Most will tell you that there are so many, and there's nothing to distinguish yours from the rest of the pack. Often they won't answer your calls or e-mails at all.

Promotions

Promotions sometimes cost money (at least for materials) and can range from sponsoring local schools to donating free nights for auctions. If you participate in auctions, you need to put limitations on the gift certificate. Most have some fine print at the bottom worded something like this: "Good for any Sunday through Thursday evening except during the month of October. Valid until December 31, 2005. Not transferable. Not exchangeable for cash." Innkeepers who do not limit certificates for auction donations always regret it.

Such donations can get you attention, but many innkeepers are now giving up on them. You will get on average one such request a week. These folks are certainly representing worthy organizations, but they don't really understand that donating a room isn't a cost-free item for you. And the tax deduction isn't really that valuable. Our best advice is to choose a few charities that you genuinely believe in, and donate your time or money rather than the inn. One good way to handle it, too, is to set aside the amount of giving (in whatever form), and settle on who will get it when you do your annual budget. Then when people call, tell them that they need to fax or e-mail you the details in time for your next budget round.

A frequent-stayer promotion may work very well for an inn in its early stages. Allow guests to accumulate credits toward a free stay by returning for a later stay or by recommending other guests who stay with you. You can even work it into the theme of your inn, as do Edd and Sally Guishard at Brookside Farm in Dulzura, California. Their guests fill up an "egg basket" to earn a free visit. How many stays are required for a free credit is up to you—at least five, probably. In any case, you need to make up some kind of formal device, such as a gift certificate with limitations, so that your free nights aren't demanded in high season. Some inns simply offer a discount on any future visit.

The principal here is a well-known retailing fact: Your best future business comes from past customers, and you need to market to them. E-mail newsletters are a good way to promote the inn to former guests. You don't want to intrude, however, or have your newsletter go into a junk mail folder. You need to do what is called "double opt-in": A visitor can sign up for the newsletter, then receives an e-mail that he or she must confirm. You can farm this out to relatively inexpensive Internet vendors like Net Office Toolbox (www.netofficetoolbox.com).

Participation in nationally run promotions can be useful—though not always. There can be a cost to those promotions that you don't recover in increased business. American Historic Inns pushes the "buy-one, get-one-free" idea very hard. In fact, AHI is very creative about promotions, and theirs are always worth looking at, even if you don't participate.

Other promotions are cooperative, and local and state associations are getting very creative about what they do. Some offer drawings for a free stay at a member inn when the guest has stayed three times at member inns—a frequent-stayer program on a state level.

Promotional ideas are as varied as the inns that run them: mystery or romantic weekends, historical events, Christmas or garden tours, and on and on. You can work promotions with any kind of group, so long as it doesn't take you too far from your main job, which is innkeeping.

Publicity

Publicity can cut two ways. If you're ready for media coverage, it's great. If you're not, it can be a disaster. If you get a magazine writer, a TV station, or a newspaper reporter to come to your inn, you cannot control what they say or write. You can't even seem to be trying.

That said, there is every reason to be grateful if a media person visits your inn. So here's some advice to help you in dealing with the media.

Reporters welcome every effort you provide to make their job easier. Give them brochures, past articles, web addresses, and phone numbers of other contacts. Be free with your quotes and access to your B&B. Offer to send supplemental information and links by e-mail.

It doesn't hurt to say nice things about the publication—everyone likes that. Send a note or e-mail after the article comes out telling them how wonderful it was, even if they misspelled your name and the name of your inn.

Suggest photo opportunities. Nothing sells an article or enhances placement on a page more than a good photo, and photos are a reader's main point of entry into an article. Don't fret about whether you've dusted lately or the curtains are a bit crooked. This isn't a shot for *Town and Country*. Also, people make photos infinitely more interesting. Don't balk about being in the photo. Better yet, suggest a photo that includes happy guests. You can offer your own photos, if they are good. Not all publications will send a photographer separately.

Be receptive to giving a writer on assignment a free stay for a night and breakfast. It costs you time and can be irksome that he or she is getting a free stay with no guarantee of a story, but in the long run, these visits should more than pay off. Usually, a writer will feel some obligation to mention you after a free or discounted stay. Some media outlets do not allow their reporters to stay free and expect a discounted rate—ask if that's the case.

Always respond to appeals for information that writers are gathering for a nationwide story. Have handy a few other story ideas—reporters like to be efficient and will sometimes mention you in more than one story if it works.

Keep in the back of your mind some peppery quotes. "I just love this business" doesn't qualify. Reporters tend to get a bit jaded about hearing the same thing from innkeepers—it may be fresh to you, but they've heard it before, and that's the kiss of death. Much better is a line like Carl's: "My worst day at innkeeping is still better than my best day in corporate life." You're selling a lifestyle here, not just antiques or breakfast.

There are editors above reporters who change stories, decide how they play, or if they even appear. Keep those guys in mind as well—they're even more suspicious than writers are, and they're always looking for a good angle or quote. If you're quotable, they'll come back to you.

Remember the old rule: "If you can't say something nice, don't say anything at all." Be positive about the inn business and about your area. You're not going to be dealing with investigative reporters trying to dig up dirt—they want happy stuff. You can certainly talk about the struggle of getting into business and the funny surprises you didn't expect but that worked out. Amusing guest stories (keeping in mind that one of them might read the story!) are always good. Make 'em laugh, make 'em cry, and they'll write about it.

Don't think just about the obvious outlets—the big-city newspaper, the largest website or TV station, or *Southern Living*. Also think of trade publications, sections of the newspaper other than travel and food, and specialty outlets of all kinds. You certainly have some special interests and read some kind of specialty publication or visit a specialty website—think about story ideas hooked to your mutual interest.

Paid Marketing

Paid marketing includes your brochure or rack card, website, printed materials, newspaper and magazine advertising, travel agent commissions, newsletters, yellow pages listings, advertising in regional publications of collateral interest (antique guides, craft and tour brochures, special events), guidebooks (now almost extinct), and the myriad websites that solicit your annual listing.

You are unlikely to be able to afford a major blitz at the outset, but that's when you need advertising the most. Generally, your marketing expenses will be about 15 percent (at least) of your annual operating budget in the early years, declining to perhaps 5 percent when you are well established. But that's only a very rough rule of thumb.

Once again, the Internet has made a considerable difference in where inn owners put their efforts. Now, as many as 80 percent of your guests will tell you that they found you on the Internet. That isn't really true; what they mean is that they looked at your inn there, but they may well have found you first through a visitors' bureau publication, a guidebook, an article, or from a colleague at work. But it's hard to trace all that back.

You can get what is called a "tracker" that tells you where visitors who come to your site are referred from. You can get a general one or one that tracks visits page by page. It's invaluable information. You should look, however, at the statistic that shows how many visitors typed your address in directly; those visitors are usually looking at some printed guide. If you are adept with your website, you can create entry pages with variations of your address, and put those variations in different outlets so that you can trace very precisely the effectiveness of your paid print advertising.

WRITING YOUR MATERIALS

The Internet has reduced brochures drastically in significance. Many, if not most, inns now use a rack card only in conjunction with a website. The website is now your major brochure, and a rack card is just that—something you put in the local welcome center and tuck into confirmation letters (if you send out a printed one rather than e-mail). Still, you are going to be writing about your inn for rack card, brochure, or website, and how you do that has not changed because of the Internet.

For any kind of material, it helps to have a professional. For website design, that's fairly obvious, but it's also true for the writing. Web guides now let you write your own copy for them, so you need a combination of written pieces: a short (25-word), a longer (50-word), and a long (100-plus-word) version of your property description.

The great thing about websites is that changes can happen instantly and updating can be constant. Not so for printed material. You'll probably have rack card runs of 10,000 copies, which can last you several years, so you want them to be right.

Your logo will be prominent on your home page, rack card, letterhead, and business card, so if you can, get a professional design. At the very least, have nice typography done of your name to serve as a logo. A good graphic artist can do either of these, as long as you can make it clear to him or her what you're trying to achieve.

Certain kinds of information are important for your website or rack card. In either or both places, you might want to include the following:

• Who the owners are and what they are like.

• What kinds of guests will feel most comfortable in your inn. (You're not really trying to appeal to everyone.)

• An accurate representation of the inn: its era, architecture, furnishings, history. Don't oversell. Don't use the word *antiques* if you don't really have them. (Antiques are defined as desirable pieces over 100 years old. Between 50 and 100 years old is semi-antique. Less than that may be old, but it isn't antique.) Never use the term *antique-filled.* If you have one queen- or king-size bed, you are not antique-filled.

• Special touches that emphasize comfort: reading lights, exceptional mattresses, modern baths, storage space, whatever.

• A sense of the menu. We used to suggest not using terms like *gourmet* or *full breakfast,* but most people understand what they mean roughly. But it does help to list some specialties.

• Any refreshments offered at times other than breakfast, such as cookies or iced tea.

• Cancellation policies, discount rates, and dates of opening or closing.

• Telephone number, address, toll-free number, website, and e-mail address. Put these in prominent places and on every page of your website.

• Area attractions that will appeal to your guests.

The writing quality of your published materials is important. You may try to write them yourself, but nonprofessionals usually fall back on clichés, copying things they like from other inns' materials. If you write your own, here are some suggestions:

Stay away from empty adjectives and clichés: *antiques, attractive, charming, country, cozy, deluxe, gourmet, elegant.* Our nominations for overused words and phrases: *nestled, antique-filled, romantic, quaint, step back in time, charm of yesterday and comforts of today,* and *quiet* (especially when it isn't). Some words that have crept in (and shouldn't have): *scrumptious, enchanting.*

In our first edition, we gave you the Brochure from Hell as an example of how not to write, full of all the sugary things that should induce diabetes in any reasonable reader. We reproduce it here with the caveat that some readers will like it and be attracted by it; nevertheless, it's better if you find your own voice rather than write in an overdone style such as this exemplifies:

> Step back in time at Scratch Inn, where a warm country welcome awaits you in our romantically restored turn-of-the-century Art Deco home. Enjoy the grand Victorian stair, our quaint rooms, our elegant period furnishings, the inviting ambience of the fireplace in our charming parlor.
>
> Guests may snuggle in front of a cozy fire in the antique-filled den, or in the summer they may enjoy a country gourmet breakfast on our charming screened porch.
>
> Pamper yourself in elegant luxury in an antique-filled sleeping chamber. Enter this romantic place of timeless tranquility and complete relaxation. Enjoy its character and charm of more than seventy-five years. Find delight in its beautiful antiques, the privacy of your lodgings, and the excellent cuisine served in an intimate atmosphere of quiet elegance. The past gently echoes throughout an elegantly restored inn that also preserves the gracious service of a bygone era. Step into history. Each visitor receives a warm welcome back to a bygone era. The casually elegant ambience is reinforced by guest bedrooms tastefully decorated with antiques and appointed with luxurious linens.

Most of these lines have been lifted from actual brochures collected over the years. No inn could be all that this one professes to be, yet inn-goers believe these descriptions. They come looking for these things, and with luck, they will find them, although often they're not there. We do love our tolerant guests who don't complain when they get less than they have been led to expect. Still, there's going to come a point—and it may be starting to happen—when some of our guests will start crying out that the emperor has no clothes.

The worst thing about this kind of drivel is that *it makes all inns sound the same.* And that's what we're trying to avoid. None of us can quite escape the clichés; we all include a few in our written materials. The best parts of many of these are the paragraphs that give the history of the particular house or its acquisition. At least give the reader a real feel for your inn. Try to be fresh.

NEWSLETTERS
Many inns create newsletters, and desktop publishing and e-mail have made putting them out much easier. Your guests, however, may not respond as much as you'd like. They see newsletters all the time, and they are solicited by e-mail so much that they may think your newsletter is yet another virus or ad for Viagra. You may be disappointed that it gets only a few responses.

In newsletters, you are writing to people who already know you, so it is especially important that your personality come through. If you are odd, the letter should be odd. If you are caring, that should come through. If you are brisk and businesslike, so should the letter be.

In fact, the term *newsletter* doesn't quite cover the kind of communication you can have with your guests. There may be almost no news in it. It is more a reminder to let your guests know you're there, and to help them recall the kind of atmosphere you have created.

One interesting phenomenon is the number of people who sign up for a newsletter on a website who have never visited your inn. Ripley has a sign-up box on his website, and his newsletter has several hundred subscribers who have never been guests!

After their first year at Rabbit Hill, John and Maureen Magee sent out a letter that brought the kind of response we would all like to have: thousands of dollars' worth of reservations. We're going to reproduce it, because it shows how wonderfully personal you can be. None of us could copy it without hitting a false note. If you are taking over a going inn, though, it should give you some idea of what you might do to make an inn your own.

To our dear guests,

We purchased Rabbit Hill 1 April 1987, with expectations of hard work and of joy greater than work. It was our expressed goal to serve you and to offer our home as yours. Today we are filled with emotion that began building upon learning that Rabbit Hill could be ours. It is our dream come true and, happily, the reality of "keeping an inn" has turned out to be even greater than the dream.

Thank you for what you have written to us. Upon closing for three weeks last November, the first thing we did was reread all the room diaries. This was overwhelming affirmation. We were filled with love. Your faces, voices, your laughter and soft conversations flooded this silent and empty inn, even if only in memory. You came here to become engaged, celebrate love, your anniversary, honeymoon, birthday, book publication, to rest, play, rediscover each other, visit colleges, visit Vermont, on business, and for reasons that are known only to you. Later so many of you wrote to us, sending pictures and more pieces of yourselves.

Maureen's favorite memories: that John could fix the commercial washing machine with auto parts on a Sunday when no one else would repair it; the people who fell asleep on the second floor porch and remained there all night.

John's favorite memories: smelling fresh baked rolls at 7 A.M.; seeing so many stars in the night sky over the lighted church steeple; soaking in the pure tranquility of the White Village in the late afternoon.

Emerson said the ornament of a house is the friends who frequent it. You have been more than guests and this house is well ornamented. Thank you all. Please join us again.

It was photocopied on letterhead, including the signatures. In other words, nothing fancy. But it was effective.

PAID ADVERTISING

Innkeepers are not good candidates for most paid advertising, except for the Internet and visitors bureau area guides. These are going to be your best bet—affordable, effective. Print advertising in magazines and newspapers is generally going to be very diluted. A message needs to be in front of a potential guest when he or she wants to see it, and more times than just once.

Regional travel magazines used to be good outlets, but even their effectiveness has diminished as their rates have gone up. If you have a million-dollar budget and a staff to administer it, then you can do extremely well. Needless to say, innkeepers do not fit that category, although we might hook on to a local attraction that does.

The advantage of the Internet is that your message is there, where it should be, when people are looking. So it makes the most sense to put your dollars there. Be cautious, however; many specialist sites might fit you (www.dogfriendly.com, for example), but they may not. Granted, you may not lose more than a hundred bucks on a nonperforming site, but those can add up quickly. The most effective broad sites at this writing are www.bedandbreakfast.com and www.bbonline.com. Your local visitors bureau guides also will be extremely effective for you, as will the websites of your local and state associations.

In effect, the Internet has replaced guidebooks. Yet the Internet has not replaced the great value of guidebooks in offering relatively unbiased opinions of inns. There is not, to our knowledge, any website that does this, though most sites offer guests a chance to sound off about places they do or do not like.

The guide to Internet guides about bed-and-breakfast inns is www.innstar.com. It rates the guides themselves, and the top-ranked ones are BedandBreakfast.com and bbonline.com. These are excellent, but they are not rankings by an independent authority; they are listings written by the innkeepers. The value of Innstar is that it tells you as an innkeeper which guides are probably going to be the best for you to buy into.

Nationwide independent rankings are done by Mobil, AAA, CAA, and a few others. These will also charge you to be listed in their guidebooks and online guides. The drawback is that they are still working to come up with ways to distinguish inns from motels. For AAA, *most* of the inns' rankings are three diamonds, which makes it difficult for the traveler to know how distinctive various inns are. It almost makes it seem that if you don't have at least three diamonds, you're not really acceptable. AAA insists that even one diamond is good, but the traveling public doesn't believe that.

State associations are taking the lead in providing guarantees to the public that their members have been inspected and meet the requirements for a safe and comfortable stay. Local associations theoretically have winnowed down their membership to include the best of the area, although there's no guarantee, but the public does at least perceive that there is some set of qualifications. The truth is that no one has yet found a way to make online guides pay the way that the guidebooks did.

TRAVEL AGENT COMMISSIONS

Travel agent commissions are a minor expense, usually 10 percent of the published rate. Unfortunately, travel agents are not fond of dealing with inns, for obvious reasons. They cannot book large blocks of rooms, where the profit really is. When they book an inn room, travel agents are usually providing a service to a client from whom they expect other business.

But as upscale clients ask for inns, business from travel agents is growing. Usually the agent is looking in the AAA book or searching online. Oddly enough, agents often seem to be less sophisticated than inn-goers in their searches.

We always pay the agent commission. It's business you wouldn't otherwise get, and prompt payment encourages an agent to use you again, especially if the client enjoyed the stay.

THE FINER POINTS OF MARKETING
Selling Your Inn over the Phone

Selling is not something most of us do naturally. But when it comes to dealing on the phone, good selling can turn the casual caller into a guest. Pay attention to how professional salespeople work the phones; they know little tricks that will work for you.

Ripley freely admits that the phone is his weakest point; he has a hard time on some days answering questions he's heard a million times. Dinie is far better at it, and here is some of her advice: Think of every caller as a potential guest, even if he or she doesn't end up staying with you. It's easy to lose your temper with a caller who asks what seem to you to be stupid questions. The old sales law is true: A happy customer will tell one or two other people; an unhappy customer will tell ten. You lose of lot of business in ways you don't know, and you may find it hard to shake a reputation for snobbishness or surliness as a result of a poor phone manner.

Some callers are easy. Their hobby is to check out every inn in the area. They often tell other people, because they like to be known as trendsetters, although now they are doing much of this online.

Referring guests to other inns is a service you perform both for other innkeepers and for guests. Local associations often require that you refer within the group exclusively, until everyone is filled. Many of these local groups also have toll-free numbers.

Because of the rise of the Internet and online booking, the telephone is dropping in importance. And it's also making many potential guests more sophisticated about the questions they ask. Most calls now begin, "I wanted to check your availability and rates." These were terms guests didn't even know ten years ago.

Little Things Mean a Lot

Here's a collection of marketing ideas that you might find useful:

- Curb appeal brings walk-in business and many lookers who wind up making reservations for a future date. How you look from the road is important. Carl and Dinie joke that a portion of maintenance and landscaping expenses belongs in the advertising budget.
- Include on your website a list of inns located elsewhere that your guests recommend. Then exchange a link from that page with the other inns.
- Swap mailing lists with a similar inn located elsewhere.
- Include a business card when you pay bills.
- Market with the local merchants' association.
- Make sure your rack cards are available where people will be looking: regional tourist offices, chambers of commerce, antique shops, interstate welcome stations.
- Invite a politician to breakfast.
- Give away extra muffins or cookies as thank-yous to referral sources, colleagues, suppliers, and such—an especially effective thing to do for the folks who volunteer at the local visitors center.
- Donate baked goods or meeting space at your inn for worthy events.
- Participate in programs such as house tours and co-op ads sponsored by trade associations.
- Write! Comment on trends, issues, stories, or anything else in the letters-to-the-editor sections of newspapers or through other media outlets.
- Offer trade discounts to your colleagues. It's a good way to learn from others, and the innkeeper can promote your inn to his or her own guests.
- Drop off a checklist of inn services with suppliers. "It's a chance to say hello and meet new staff people who are potential referral sources," says Carl, who also includes some of the Wedgwood's home-baked goodies.
- Fill rooms at the last minute with creative, value-added, online promotions and specials.

Act Collectively

It is useful for innkeepers to start to think about a future that is bound to change. Guests expect even small companies to act professionally. That does not mean that you lose your folksiness or individuality, but there is nothing to be gained in trying to do everything yourself.

Through associations or loose arrangements with other inns, you should start working toward group marketing, if the inns have not already put together a local association. These local groups are bound to grow more and more important. In Asheville, for example, the Asheville Bed and Breakfast Association has grown to the point that the city planning department does not consider any regulation change without consulting the organization. The association has gone so far as to propose a city license for inns, and the city may well act on it.

Local associations not only do joint marketing, but they also can put together meetings that would not be possible for one inn, using the whole group. More on this in chapter 10.

Never Overlook an Opportunity

Marketing means seeing opportunities in circumstances where no one else would. There's no way to predict what or when these will be.

Crescent Dragonwagon, a legendary innkeeper and chef who started the Dairy Hollow House in Eureka Springs, Arkansas, is a phrase magician, beginning with her own name, which she created in the 1960s. For the inn's restaurant, she invented the term "Nouveau Zarks" cuisine. How can guests resist?

Pat O'Brien, whose Blue Spruce Inn in Soquel, California, has been open since 1990, went through an expansion shortly thereafter. He took an opportunity most of us would miss: "I learned quite by accident how far fresh-baked cookies, hot coffee, and a few encouraging words can go. . . . We had a great deal of reconstruction done on the house involving many different workers from a wide variety of professions. We also did business with many suppliers. With each new contract, whether it was the tile setter, fixture salesperson, or carpet installer, I personally praised the quality of their work or product. My original goal was to share our dream with them in the hopes of inspiring them to do their best work. What I didn't bargain for was that these craftspeople became ambassadors for our fledgling inn. They sent referrals to us, told their friends about us, and made reservations for themselves in favorite rooms they had worked on. It was a wonderful experience."

The most important thing in marketing your inn is to depend on and listen to your guests. In the end, they will be your best ambassadors, critics, customers, and marketers.

7

Policies and Procedures: Save Yourself a Lot of Grief

"AN ABSOLUTE RULE FOR INNKEEPERS IS TO SET POLICY AND STICK BY IT."

—Arna Fay

Your policies make it possible for you to offer the kind of service that gives your inn its special character. As much as your amenities, they help define your inn. They are an expression of your personality and will vary accordingly. There are no right or wrong policies, though all should be based on principles of hospitality. Your policies should not be arbitrary; they're for the guests' good as well as yours. Guests are happier if they are not left wondering what they may or may not do.

In our discussion of policies and procedures, we use several terms that it may be useful to define here:

Minimum stay: A requirement (usually during the busiest season) that guests stay a minimum number of nights.

Comp: Complimentary—a free night given for publicity or for other reasons you deem important.

Seasons: High season is your busiest, off-season your slowest. These are joined by the "shoulder" season.

Guest: A paying customer, often referred to as a houseguest, reservation, or overnight lodger. Not a patient, client, or fare. An individual guest you know rather than an anonymous room number at a large hotel.

Confirmed reservation: A reservation accompanied by advance deposit or guaranteed by a valid credit card number.

Cancellation policy: A policy that governs a guest cancellation of a confirmed or guaranteed reservation.

POLICIES AND PROCEDURES MANUAL

Like a child who asks a question of both parents and chooses the answer he likes better, a guest may do the same with you, your partner, and your staff. You want everyone singing from the same choir book. That's why it's important to have house rules. Your policy manual also will be important for your innsitter or staff in your absence. You want them to run your inn just as you would, but they cannot if you haven't explained things clearly.

By policy manual, we don't mean an encyclopedic tome that is intimidating to look at. A simple three-ring notebook with index tabs will do. It should contain all the policies and procedures that are in force in your inn, as well as your ways of handling the many small details of managing the "back of the house," such as the location of the electrical panel box. It might even have a section on restaurants, attractions, and other information about the area. Keep several copies, and note changes, additions, and revisions in every copy as they occur. Although an online version of your manual is nice, you need to have backup paper copies in the event of a power outage. Be sure to include the name and phone number of your electrician.

Other things to include are miscellaneous housekeeping details, such as where you keep soaps, sheets, and cleaning supplies; any peculiarities about any parts of the house or the grounds; and vendors and maintenance contractors. A section on how to handle an emergency or accident, from a fall to a flood, as well as emergency contact information is also a necessity.

Many things that you learn as you go along become automatic. If you forget to pass that knowledge along to others, they have to reinvent the wheel. In large organizations, this is known as institutional memory, and companies regularly lose it, to their cost. Small as you are, communication problems and lapses can create exactly the same problems for which we blame large bureaucracies. At least they have the excuse of bigness.

COMMUNICATING POLICIES TO GUESTS

Both your website and your brochure should include a dated rate schedule, any restrictions (such as minimum stays), check-in and check-out times, deposit and cancellation policies, kinds of payment accepted, house rules on pets and smoking, and any other policies that are important to you. Surf the web and look at other brochures, as many as you can, to get an idea of the kinds of things that can be included.

Many guests, however, are referred to you before they ever view your website or read your brochure. You must convey your policies to them in a way that will not be forbidding—you do want them to come! When the telephone call comes for reservations, mention policies such as restrictions on smoking or small children to determine whether the guest is right for your inn.

Although an inn doesn't usually post its regulations on the back of a room door as motels do, we can still communicate our policies to our guests. You might use an attractive script note, nicely framed and placed on a bureau or hung on the wall. A pleasantly written welcoming letter with the guest's name on it (that helps to ensure that it is read) is another method. Include not only your rules, but also any interesting historic tidbits about the house and the area.

Still another way to do this is with a room book, a nicely tabbed compendium of information about the inn, your policies, what to do in case of fire, local restaurants and attractions, and so forth. This is much more elaborate and can take quite a bit of time to create and update.

Some inns, like the Meldrum Bay Inn on Manitoulin Island in Ontario, Canada, incorporate their policies into their reservation confirmation letters, which they e-mail or send to their guests at the time of booking. At other inns, the innkeeper offers a tour at check-in, during which the rules are covered verbally (a tour is always a good idea anyway).

How you communicate your house rules depends on the type of guest you are dealing with and your price range. The higher your rates, the less appropriate are room notes.

SETTING YOUR POLICIES

Now, what sorts of policies should you have? Some situations are so common that you can't avoid them. You need to know in advance how you are going to handle guests who do not follow those policies. The most important ones deal with reservations, deposits, and cancellations, but there are a number of others.

Cancellations and No-Shows

Every innkeeper dreads cancellations and no-shows. Inns are unlike other lodging properties in that we don't (or at least shouldn't) overbook. The quid pro quo is this: We promise a reserved guest space, and the guest promises to arrive. But they don't always show up, nor do they always understand that you can't be flexible about last-minute cancellations in the way that a large property (that does overbook) might be.

Cancellations and no-shows are often the worst for inns in heavily touristed areas. Telling the truth and curb appeal can make a difference. If a guest feels that he or she has been lied to about what to expect, and your inn does not look cozy, elegant, charming, secluded, grand, or whatever epithet you've attached to it, then that guest may well drive on. And you may be out of luck.

"Make sure your cancellation policy is explicit," says Richard Carlson, former owner of Savannah's Ballastone Inn. "Guests have a million excuses for why they need to cancel on the day of arrival. Make sure you are inflexible on this rule, or you will lose your shirt."

Here is a typical reservation sequence:

October 1: The guest calls and makes a reservation for the beginning of November. You pencil in the reservation and tell the guest that a deposit check must be received by mail within one week, or the reservation will be erased from the book. You send the guest a brochure.

October 6: The check arrives. You indicate this in the book.

October 7: You mail a confirmation letter to the guest.

There are other ways of handling this sequence. Most inns now allow reservations to be held with a credit card number and charge the deposit to that card immediately. Reservation programs also can tell you if you've been given a valid card. This is similar to the way hotels hold reservations, and guests understand it. Yet other inns require an advance deposit of one night or 50 percent at the time of booking, whether by telephone or e-mail. The confirmation letters should go out to these guests at once, by snail mail or e-mail.

At all times, you should send a brochure or e-mail with an introductory letter to the guest, reiterating your important policies. If you require an advance deposit by check or money order a certain time before the reservation date, state that policy. You can do so pleasantly, but do it.

Here's an example of a confirmation letter that, with the appropriate alterations, can serve as an introductory letter that you send by regular mail or e-mail:

Dear Confirmed Guest,

We're looking forward to welcoming you to Scratch Inn for the three nights of October 2, 3, and 4. We've reserved the Lilac Room for you as requested: a second-floor room with a queen-size bed and private bath (with tub) at $125 per night, plus tax. We'll do all we can to make your anniversary celebration special. Your planned arrival time of 6 P.M. is fine; if you expect to arrive at a different time, please let us know so that your room can be ready.

We will expect your deposit check of $187.50 (50 percent of the total amount) by September 15, or we cannot hold the accommodation. [*Alternatively:* Your reservation is guaranteed by your credit card number; *or,* Your credit card has been charged for the deposit.] If you wish to cancel or change this reservation, we must receive notice of the change by 2 P.M., September 25. We will return your deposit [*or,* We will issue a credit slip] less a $20 handling fee if we are able to rebook the room. Your balance of $187.50, plus applicable sales and occupancy tax on your total stay, is due upon arrival [*or,* due on departure].

We serve afternoon tea to all guests at 5 P.M. each day. We always have an interesting group of guests, and many friendships have been made here. Please be reminded that we do not permit smoking at Scratch Inn. If you have any questions, the enclosed brochure will answer many of them [*or,* click on the hyperlink to view our website and your guest room], but don't hesitate to call if others occur to you.

Such a communication makes it clear that the deposit will be held in the event of a cancellation. Your inn's policies on how much of the deposit to return, or whether to charge for only one night, may vary. We think you should assess a $15 to $50 handling charge, no matter what the reason, for a cancellation outside the specified time, to cover the expenses of providing a refund and all the other nuisance that goes with a canceled reservation. Some inns do not refund the deposit and instead apply it to a future date, issuing a gift certificate.

Brochures and websites are a good place to state how you handle refunds. Here is how the brochure of Sunny Pines Bed & Breakfast in Harwich West, Massachusetts, does it:

1. Deposit must be received within one week from when you call to make a reservation.
2. Entire amount is requested for stays of less than seven nights, one-half payment for longer stays. The deposit then applies to last days with balance due payable upon arrival.
3. Deposit will be happily refunded or applied to a new date if the cancellation is received two weeks prior to arrival date. If not, we will do our best to fill your room, and if successful, we will return your deposit, less a $25 han-

dling fee. No refund on early departure. Ten percent service charge for credit card cancellations.

4. Your canceled check or credit card slip is your receipt.

A really tough situation is when a guest cancels on check-in day because of an illness or accident. That's no problem if you're able to rebook to a walk-in, but you can't count on it. You'll have to consult your own softheartedness, but consider that you and your inn deserve not to be sacrificed to the whim, or even misfortunes, of a guest. Remember what Richard Carlson says about losing your shirt.

A no-show is the most awful experience for innkeepers. Until it happens to you, you cannot imagine how bad it is. Why? If you have only five rooms, and two couples don't show up, you've just lost 40 percent of your revenue for that day! This perishable commodity cannot be recovered. So you sit and wait for hours, wondering what happened and why, and what to do.

If you collected a deposit, it's not a total loss. If you don't have that, you can try sending out a bill. Good luck on collecting. If someone is ill-mannered enough not to show up without an explanation, what likelihood is there that he or she will pay any attention to a bill?

Another way to deal with no-shows is to use a credit card guarantee. Some companies and banks are better about this than others. We believe that card companies are too willing to charge back to the inn on the mere word of a guest. After all, they want to keep the card holder as their customer. You should always find out what the policy is for Visa and MasterCard through the bank you intend to use. If you follow its rules, the bank should be willing to extend the guarantee. If not, look for another bank or credit card processing company. American Express and Discover will also issue the guarantee. The usual rule is that a guest is a no-show after 6 P.M. the day of check-in, and the card companies will honor that.

If a guest cancels without enough notice but has reserved the room with a credit card number, issue that guest a cancellation number, and write it on the cancelled reservation. You create the number, so it doesn't matter what the number is, as long as you keep a record of it. If you then charge the guest because the room was not rebooked, and the guest refuses the charge, you can ask the credit card company if the guest used that cancellation number. If the guest did, then you have proof that the guest in fact made the reservation. It's a wee bit of trickery, but it's a legitimate weapon against the inconsiderate types who make your life miserable. If your cancellation policy is clear and in writing, and you have made a practice of tracking in this way—and if it doesn't happen very often—you have some leverage with the card companies.

Another method is to charge the guest when he or she makes the reservation. The credit card companies' point-of-purchase processing machines allow you to punch a credit card number or swipe the card and get the money immediately. If the charge is refused, you may still have a problem, though. Some guests attempt to get out of a charge by exaggerating or making up deficiencies.

If you don't accept credit cards, you have no way to guarantee last-minute reservations when there is no time to receive a deposit. If those guests don't show, you're out of luck. Even the smallest inns should take some cards; very few do not accept them today. If you want business travelers, you'll almost certainly have to accept American Express. AE used to be rather difficult to deal with for small inns, but that has changed dramatically in recent years, and the company is often better about backing inns than Visa and MasterCard are.

One chilling new wrinkle in this age of late-reserving guests: Some card companies are using the "buyer's remorse" option from contract law. This option allows buyers three days after signing a contract to change their minds and get their deposit back. We can only hope this new practice of interpreting a room reservation as a contract in this manner does not catch on.

Asking for Your Money

New innkeepers are sometimes a bit shy about asking for payment. Common advice is that you should request payment on check-in. In most cases, that's a good idea, but again, your ambience should dictate what you do. If you want your guests to feel like friends on a visit, you might prefer to request payment on checkout. Guests often feel more comfortable about paying then, especially when their stay has been pleasant.

On the other hand, there are rare occasions when someone walks out without paying. This happens mostly in homestays and smaller B&Bs. It is therefore a good policy to have a credit card guarantee on every guest. You can use the card machine to see if a credit card is good for the amount of the stay, and even put a hold on that amount to guarantee that you will be paid when the time comes.

We have found that in the smaller inn, it works to give the guest a bill at the final breakfast—rather like a restaurant does. But this doesn't work very well for larger properties.

Children
Children around an inn can be your own or your guests'. One of the demographic trends that began in the 1990s is older couples with children. These couples like to do things as a family, creating a ticklish problem for innkeepers.

Many inn-goers will not be happy in an inn where there are children. Yet if you systematically exclude children, you may run afoul of laws protecting the civil rights of minorities (yes, children are people too). Many innkeepers are becoming concerned about this possibility, although to date we have not heard of any suits.

It is not an easy dilemma to resolve, but there are solutions. Once again, you must come back to what kind of inn you are trying to create and how you convey that to potential guests.

First of all, there is business—quite a lot, we think—to be gained from accepting children, if you can manage it well. Make it clear in your policies with a line that says, "Children welcome with advance notification." Potential guests will be alerted that there may be children in residence, and they can make plans accordingly. Inns that accept families have to make sure they have such things as cribs, rollaway cots for the parents' rooms, and childproof sleeping and public rooms. Fred

Strout of Applewood Colonial Inn in Williamsburg, Virginia, even offers baby-sitting services to guests.

But what about those many inns that present themselves as romantic retreats? Their ambience—and much of their business—could be lost if they accepted children.

If you are not an inn that can deal with children, you need to let people know that with a statement such as "The inn is not suitable for small children," "The inn has no activities for children," or "Small children find us boring." Such a statement will alert families to the fact that your inn may not be appropriate for them. Or you can state quite frankly that children are incompatible with your ambience, as Seacrest Manor does: "For the comfort of our guests, and as our accommodations are limited, we cannot accept reservations for children under 16 or for groups."

Pricing can serve to encourage or discourage bringing children. Making no distinction in rates between children and adults gives guests reasonable notice that you are not family-oriented. You may also say, "Only two persons per room." A couple traveling with a child would thus have to book two rooms, and the cost would be prohibitive to most families.

The tone of your brochure also should convey whether you are suitable for children. Mentioning antiques (please don't say "antique-filled") will often tip travelers off. And the travel guidebooks and online directories are excellent about letting their readers know whether you are child-friendly.

People usually are good about asking if children are welcome when they call for reservations. Be honest in your response.

Let's digress for a moment into the area of discrimination and civil rights. Smaller properties are unlikely to face lawsuits charging them with discrimination. It is an extremely rare person who feels he or she must sue on a matter of principle. Such a person would have to be determined to bring a child to an inn—and it's far cheaper to get a baby-sitter for one weekend. Courts likely will avoid such cases, knowing that you have to be able to create the kind of business that will bring in income. You are not required to destroy your own living.

You do not, of course, want to even arouse the possibility of a lawsuit. There probably is such a person out there, and all you can do to protect yourself is to take reasonable precautions. The reasonable precaution in this case is to avoid putting a line in your brochure that says, "We don't take children." Most state and regional inn associations advise against outright bans; use the means we have suggested to discourage children if your inn is not appropriate for them.

There was a time when children did travel well. And many children still do. As Dinie says, "There are no bad children, only bad parents." Some parents create problems for all families when they fail to notice or deal with the disturbances their children create for others. Alas, many innkeepers have gotten stuck baby-sitting, as thoughtless parents dumped their children and escaped for an afternoon or evening. This is not part of the deal, and innkeepers should firmly refuse such responsibilities, if for no other reason than the insurance considerations. If you do get stuck, at least add a baby-sitting charge.

Most innkeepers will accept children on a slow night. If a parent really wants to bring a child to your inn, you might suggest a midweek visit in the slow season. Dinie says this is our chance to educate the next generation of inn-goers—an idea we all need to consider seriously. Children are often delightful guests. You cannot predict their behavior any more than you can an adult guest's. I was skeptical when one parent wanted to bring her nine-year-old daughter to the Inn on Montford, but the parent said, "Oh, she's better behaved than I am!" The little girl was a pleasure. She enjoyed the house and never disturbed the other guests. The best solution is to set rules that apply to all guests, regardless of age: no running, loud parties, disturbing other guests, destroying inn property, and so forth. If anyone of any age breaks your rules, out they go. You are then enforcing behavior, not discriminating because of age.

Carl and Dinie have kept track of how many child guests from the 1980s have returned to their Wedgwood Inns as adults. In 2003, forty-six guests (representing more than 120 room-nights), aged twenty-one to thirty, had first stayed at the inn as children. For the first nine months of 2004, the number was already forty-two and growing. And many of these folks are returning with children of their own. "Not a bad way to build a business with a strong repeat clientele," Dinie says with a smile. "We don't accept more than one family traveling at a time, and we book them in either our separate carriage house or three-room suite with kitchenette." A number of inns are taking this approach very successfully; a kitchenette appeals to parents, who are often on a budget, and relieves you of the worry of having children at the table.

Pets

For a number of reasons, most inns cannot accept pets. That's unfortunate, since pets can be pleasant traveling companions. Europeans frequently take their pets along on trips. It is not against French or English restaurant health codes to allow animals in dining rooms, and in those countries, one often sees a diner with his dog under the table.

American health departments frown on this practice, and American pet owners often make matters worse by not training their pets properly. This makes for trouble for inn owners who would like to accept pets. Cats with their claws can ruin your linens, draperies, and upholstery. Pets with urinary problems or poor house training can be even more destructive.

Another serious problem is allergies. Many guests are allergic to animals, particularly cats. It isn't fair to make them miserable because there are pets around. For this reason, if you have pets of your own, keep them out of guest rooms. If you aren't going to enforce this, make potential guests aware of that beforehand.

Some guests have phobias about certain kinds of animals. We have had guests who were afraid of our pets, and we had to take care to keep them apart. These fears are irrational; there's no point in arguing about them. You do not want an unhappy guest, so your pets—which are wonderfully entertaining to most guests—must be kept out of sight of people who fear them.

If you do have pets of your own, this may be an additional reason to keep guests' pets out of your inn. Established animals don't always take well to newcomers. This is part of the vicious circle: Because Americans don't travel often with their pets, their pets often don't travel well.

The simplest policy is to put "Pets not accepted" in your brochure, and handle specific cases as they come up. You can offer to find a place at a nearby kennel for the animals. If you find yourself dealing with many pets, you may be able to negotiate a special rate at a particular kennel in exchange for sending all your guests' pets there. If guests bring their cats in cages—and promise to keep them there—you might allow them in the rooms. Of course, keep in mind that the owners might break their promises.

Those establishments that do accept a pet usually charge an extra nightly fee in the range of $20 to $30 to cover the cost of extra cleaning. These inns may limit the type (no snakes, please!) and size of the pet, require proof that the animals' shots are up-to-date, and require that the pet be kept in a travel cage. To keep the problem of allergies to a minimum, usually one specific guest room is set aside for use by pet owners, and the pet is restricted from the public spaces at the inn. "Pet owners are some of our most loyal repeat guests and give many word-of-mouth referrals," says Dinie. "However, to avoid an avalanche of dogs at the inn, we do not advertise on any of the online directories geared toward pet owners. And as with our policy regarding children, we allow only one pet at the inn on any given night. Balance is the key."

At Biltmore Village Inn, we have one room in the outlying cottage that is for visiting pets. We are finding that more and more people want to bring their dogs (oddly, very few cats), and these dogs in general have been excellent guests. So this is a good market.

Check-in and Checkout Times

These are not trivial matters. You cannot always be in the inn, and you may not always have an assistant there. You have to have some time to clean rooms, attend meetings, update your website, make in-person marketing visits, shop for supplies, go to the bank or post office, or do any of a number of other things that have to be done to keep your inn running.

If you allow guests to check in and out at any time, you'll find yourself with the previous night's guests still visiting with you or one another, unprepared rooms, and no hope of getting it all organized. You must manage the flow of traffic through your inn in order to operate efficiently. If you don't, you'll seem harried and will spoil the ambience. The next stage is innkeeper burnout.

Allow yourself a minimum of half an hour per room for cleaning. If you have eight rooms, you should allow four uninterrupted hours between regular checkout and check-in. That way, if your maids don't show and you have to change the whole house yourself, you can get it done in time for your next set of guests.

With any luck, this will never happen, but innkeepers can count on Murphy's Law and all of its corollaries. Be quite strict about this policy, because guests often say they want to check in at certain times without following through. You might on occasion allow a noon check-in, only to find yourself waiting around for hours for a guest who doesn't arrive until 4 P.M. That sort of thing can put you in a bad mood, and you're not likely to be a good host if you're in a bad mood.

One useful solution is offered by the ubiquitous cell phone. You might ask your guests to call a few minutes before arriving, so that you can be doing other things in the meantime.

Smoking

Even as late as 1987, it was rather daring to forbid smoking. Today it's easier. Because only 30 percent of the population smokes, 70 percent of your potential guests prefer to be in a nonsmoking environment.

For safety, health, and maintenance reasons, most inns today are nonsmoking, and most guests expect it. Put your smoking policy in your brochure and website, and state it on the phone. Let guests know this policy early; why go through the entire reservation spiel for nothing? At Wedgwood, after the availability of a requested date is confirmed, the next information given is that the inn is a smoke-free establishment: no smoking, no candles, and no incense either. At Biltmore Village Inn, we have a policy of no smoking in the inn or on the grounds near the house. People find that surprising, but smoke does drift. Hard-core smokers use their cars.

Nevertheless, there are guests who do smoke in rooms any way, and these are often hard-core, unrepentant smokers. Keep track of who did it—and you will know—and make sure you do not allow that guest to return. You can also try to charge that guest's credit card for the cost of cleaning that room of smoke. We know of one inn-sitter who went so far as to call the police when a smoker refused to stop. Many innkeepers put a sign in each room that says, "Thank you for not smoking," along with a notice that there is a substantial charge—usually more than $250—for smoking in a room.

If you do allow smoking, let nonsmokers know in advance. You could also set aside nonsmoking rooms and certainly a nonsmoking sitting area.

Breakfast Service

Inns serve breakfast in many different ways and at many different times. Some serve everyone together at a fixed time. Some set a range of times for breakfast service. Some serve breakfast in bed or put trays outside the room. Some serve coffee and pastries quite late. Much depends on what you can do and what you're trying to accomplish in the way of ambience.

You should make quite clear how you do your breakfasts and what you expect of guests. Because she cannot seat everyone at once, Margaret Perry, former owner of the Thomas Shepherd Inn, used to have her guests sign up for a particular time the night before.

Other innkeepers have guests sign up for when they want tray delivery to their rooms. Some inns have specialties that are timed and cannot be kept warm. Guests are informed that the time is not flexible, but that the breakfast is worth the trouble of being there at a particular time.

Tea and Afternoon Refreshments

Serving your guests beverages or light snacks in the late afternoon provides an opportunity for your guests to get to know you and each other. It also gives you a chance to try your culinary skills on something other than breakfast.

Should you provide alcoholic beverages? Generally not. There are host liability consequences, and local ordinances might not permit it. Providing drinks can be quite expensive as well.

Guests often bring their own alcohol or food. They may want to keep their provisions in your refrigerator. How you handle this is up to you. Providing access to an under-the-counter-size refrigerator in a public space (not the inn kitchen) for guest use is a common practice. Many inns now offer a guest pantry with access to a coffee machine. There are superb machines that can provide one-cup brewing of coffee or tea, and most bottled water machines have both hot and cold water taps.

You may not want to allow your guests to bring food or beverages into your inn, or you may want to restrict where they can take their goodies. People eating in their rooms will cause cleaning problems. Many guests won't ask your permission; they'll just do it.

Afternoon tea and refreshments can help discourage in-room gourmands. If you offer your guests a snack yourself, they'll be less likely to sneak one later in their rooms.

Public and Private Space

You need to make clear to guests where they may freely roam. The inn is your home, and you ought to keep some parts of it to yourself, no matter how generous you are.

King's Cottage in Lancaster, Pennsylvania, has a nice little sign: "Please respect closed doors." That covers several bases. Guests often want to look at other rooms, but you can't have them walking in on other guests!

Some innkeepers are happy to have guests in their kitchens and may even invite them in. Others don't like it, or their insurance company or local health department doesn't allow it. If you want to keep guests out of the kitchen, put a "Private" or "Please knock" sign on the door. Cassandra Clark of the Secret Garden in Weaverville, North Carolina, has a sign that says, "If you're in this kitchen, you'd better be cooking."

Few guests will abuse these rules; the ones who do should be politely but firmly corrected: "I'm sorry. Guests are not allowed in this area. If you'll step into the parlor, I'll be glad to take care of any request." Of course, you need to make it possible for guests to find you easily, so that they aren't inclined to go poking into areas they should stay out of.

Tipping

As you add staff, tipping becomes a ticklish question. A few guests do leave tips in the rooms as a matter of course, and they are often generous ones. But most guests do not.

Encouraging tipping can be one way to get the kind of chamber help you need. It may, however, lead to a potential clash with guests. If you leave envelopes for tips in the rooms, they will feel they are being charged something that they weren't told about. On the other hand, without that extra income for the cleaners, you may end up on the thin edge of profitability—things can be that tight.

One solution is to include the service charge on the bill. Many upscale inns are doing this. The gratuity is added on just as the sales tax is. Guests are informed ahead of time. Handling it that way seems to cause less offense. Seacrest Manor puts an attractive card in the rooms that reads: "Many of our guests have suggested that it is less confusing and fairer to add the gratuities to the bill. Therefore, a charge of ten percent of the basic room rate will be included on your bill and distributed to the appropriate staff members."

8

Attention to Detail: No Inn Is Great without It

"IN THIS BUSINESS, AN INNKEEPER WHO IS NOT ORGAN-
IZED IS DONE FOR."

—Annette King

Good innkeeping is in the details and how you handle them. You will come to appreciate just how many details there are as you go along. You can get lost in the details, or you can use them to make your inn's statement—something that larger lodging properties cannot do.

Although no detail is unimportant, some are more important than others. Of them all, the most important is cleanliness. Says Helen Goodbrod of Ye Olde Library Bed & Breakfast in Jersey Shore, Pennsylvania, "Details in innkeeping that are most essential are a clean home, clean bed linens, lots of clean towels, and air-conditioning in the summertime." Reasonable warmth in the winter, with lots of quilts and blankets for snuggling on chilly nights, is also expected. Guests like to read in bed, so there should be good lighting (at least 100 watts) on both sides.

Private baths are no longer considered an amenity. Edward Mahoney, a tourist extension specialist at Michigan State

University, led a university-funded study of B&B clientele in Michigan. A major conclusion of the study was that most guests who shared a bathroom would have preferred a private one. Most guests who had private baths said they would not have stayed in a B&B if the room had not had one. Most guests also said they would pay extra for a private bath. Many pay extra for larger, luxury bathrooms too.

But much of the detail in inns isn't what you provide; it's how you provide it. Knowing what you want to offer and what kinds of guests you will host help you stay on top of the details that will make your inn successful.

COMMUNICATIONS

Peg McCabe of the Queen Anne Inn in Newport, Rhode Island, says that good telephone skills are essential to operating a successful inn. "I spend a lot of money on ads and direct mail to generate telephone calls from prospective guests. To ensure that that money's well spent, I answer the phone promptly and at all hours. I can also 'read' people over the phone, weeding out those callers I think wouldn't like what my inn offers."

Dinie at Wedgwood agrees. "Callers and e-mailers have told me I have the ability to 'smile' over the phone and the internet and establish an easy rapport with them. I have never tried to convert a Holiday Inn-goer to our B&B. If a prospective guest really wants a forty-eight-inch in-room television or champagne glass-shaped whirlpool bathtub, then I refer that caller elsewhere. We want only happy guests at our inn. Being able to discern people's needs and wants over the telephone or Internet is critical in screening out those who would be unhappy at our inn."

Inns cannot afford to let telephone callers and website surfers slip away. Except for drop-in business, all initial guest contacts are by phone or e-mail. Unless you have an 800 number, it's the caller's dime; whichever it is, you should be willing to spend as much time on the phone as they are. Here are some useful telephone and e-mail tips:

- Answer the telephone within the first three rings. Take a slow, deep breath before you answer; this will help you speak slowly and clearly. Your voice should be pleasant, conveying a genuine interest in assisting the caller. After a greeting, identify yourself as the innkeeper and give your name. The first thirty seconds are the most important in making an impression.

- Check your e-mail at least three times a day.
- Smile as you answer; somehow that smile projects itself through the line and across the World Wide Web.
- You should demonstrate knowledge of your inn and what it offers, but be a reservation taker, not just an information giver. Try to find out exactly what the person is looking for; don't just give facts about the inn.
- Address the person by name, if he or she gives it to you.
- Keep your telephone conversation flowing, especially while you look up information.
- Never leave a caller on hold for long periods.
- Offer alternatives—such as alternate dates, referrals to other inns, or relevant links—if you cannot meet the person's needs.
- Repeat any information the person gives you for clarity and completeness.
- Return calls and messages as soon as possible.
- If you will not be replying to e-mail for several days, create a message or automatic response stating such, and give a telephone number that the e-mailer can use instead.

Answering Machines or Voice Mail

Voice mail can be a godsend to the harried innkeeper, if used properly. But many callers hate it; leaving recorded messages makes them feel self-conscious. They may also feel that they are being treated impersonally—the last impression you want them to have. So how do you overcome these problems?

First of all, don't feel guilty. If you have a small property, you cannot afford to be on call twenty-four hours a day. You can't afford it in wear and tear on yourself, and you can't afford an all-night desk clerk. Potential guests who expect you to take reservations at 3 A.M. are not guests you want anyway.

There are right ways to use voice mail, however. The message should be clear, and there should be sufficient time for a potential guest to leave a message. Nothing is more irritating than to be cut off in midmessage. Since there is the possibility that a guest is calling at 3 A.M. because of an emergency, the message should include an emergency number for off hours.

Online reservation systems have not replaced the need for a good voice mail message for callers. All of them allow the caller to interrupt the message and begin recording his or her own. A very long and complete description of the inn on the outgoing message, beginning with "You may interrupt this tape and leave a message by pressing the asterisk on your phone." is a good practice. Some guests will call back to listen to the message several times. It will make them more comfortable about making reservations (there are, believe it or not, many people who are nervous about calling for reservations). Now that we have the Internet, this is less critical, but many inn-goers still are not comfortable with making reservations online.

Toll-Free Numbers and Cell Phones

Almost all reservation calls are going toll-free these days, so it's important to have a toll-free number. They are not overwhelmingly expensive and will get you calls from travel agents who won't call an inn otherwise. Even the smallest inn should consider one of these. You often can choose the number, depending on your carrier. Try to get a toll-free number that uses your main number digits, with the only difference being the prefix.

For your own convenience, you also need a cell phone to which you can transfer your main number when you are out of the inn. You'll take lots of reservations in the grocery store.

Fax Machines and Guest Computers

Fax machines are as common in today's inns as telephones. Many innkeepers have combination scanner/copier/fax machines or fax capability through their computers. If you are trying to encourage bookings from business travelers or corporate clients, a fax machine is a must for their business communication. With all the viruses and spyware flying around the

Internet, the old-fashioned fax machine still has its uses. You will also find fax machines useful for travel agent confirmations and standard reservation forms, especially for last-minute callers who don't have e-mail.

Now that so many guests are wanting to check their e-mail or log into the company computer at a distance, many inns are offering Internet connections or access to a computer. Given how cheap computers are, and how easy it is to create a network, this is not a bad idea. A wireless access point (WAP) will usually accomplish the same thing for computer-savvy guests.

Answering the Mail

Speed in responding to written communications is essential. The late Leighton Saville, innkeeper at Seacrest Manor in Rockport, Maine, said: "Twenty minutes after our mail is delivered, the postal truck swings past our house again to deliver to the other side of the street. We try to answer our guest mail fast enough to have it ready for that returning mail truck. Not only is the speedy handling of our mail appreciated by our guests, but it also helps us obtain new business by being the first to respond to a prospective guest's inquiry. It may be a small detail, but it counts."

Today it is common practice for innkeepers to send e-mail confirmations to their guests, even if the guests' initial contact was by telephone or regular mail, because it is faster, more efficient, and less costly. (No paper or postage stamp!) Nicole Lavigne of the Quebec House Inn in Canada also points out that this way, "We also have their e-mail addresses for future marketing opportunities."

RESERVATION RECORD KEEPING

If you don't keep careful track of reservations, you won't be in the business long. There are successful innkeepers who still do not have a reservation book or an online calendar, but we suspect that they are successful in spite of themselves.

Professionally run inns have separate portfolios, or forms, paper or electronic, or slips for each guest. The information you include on the forms should have a purpose, so that you don't hold people on the phone unnecessarily long. The following information should be included:

Current date
Dates of reservation
Guest name(s)
Address
Day, evening, and cell phone numbers
E-mail address
Room assigned
Room rate quoted (perhaps discounted, or seasonally adjusted)
Credit card number (if appropriate)
Date deposit is due or taken (if appropriate)
How the guest was referred to you
Time of arrival
Notes

All of this information is important to you. You might keep your payment records on the reservation form as well. Also consider including a checklist to make sure you have mentioned important policy or comfort issues: no smoking, dietary restrictions, cancellation, check-out time, and so on.

After you have acknowledged each reservation with a confirmation letter or e-mail, file the slip by scheduled date of arrival. Paper backup is important to have, even if the reservation request came via the Internet; print out the Webervations or e-mail request. The simplest file system is a file box divided by month, with day dividers in the current month. Keep moving the day dividers to the next month, rearranging future cards as you go.

Once made, reservations must be booked. Pencil them into your reservation book, or upload them into your electronic calendar. This can be as simple as a customized week-at-a-glance calendar, or it can be more complex, with space to note the deposit received and the time of arrival. Even a large inn does not need a computer software program to keep track of its reservations, so don't sweat if you are not comfortable with reservation software.

Financially successful innkeepers spend a lot of thought on how to take reservations, with the goal to book as many room-nights as possible. The strategy? Use policies such as minimum length of stay to piece together your reservation book puzzle. For example, if you have a six-room urban inn, don't book all its available rooms for a weekday night with only single-night stays, as there is a good chance a businessperson will call closer to the date, requesting a multiple-night stay. Similarly, if you have a college inn with strong weekend business, don't book the whole house for only one weekend night if Monday is a legal holiday, as you're likely to receive requests for three-night stays for that weekend.

You can buy reservation books or make up your own. The sample from a reservation book shown on page 132 has the rooms arranged vertically, but you can as easily arrange them horizontally and the days vertically. You can create such a reservation form on your computer and print it out as needed, or draw it by hand and then photocopy it. Punch holes in the pages, and put them in a three-ring notebook with page dividers for the months.

Some innkeepers suggest that you keep a second, easily portable, week-at-a-glance reservation book that merely notes occupancy so that you can take reservations on the run. You need to keep it synchronized with your print or electronic reservation book. You have to decide what fits your style and degree of organization.

Sally Blumberg of Sunday's Mill Farm in Bernville, Pennsylvania, is supremely well organized: "I have found it important to have a separate calendar for reservations. I have an information card on each guest so that I can record dates of all calls, brochure and confirmation mailings, and check numbers. I even take photos of my guests to help me remember them when they call for later reservations." New reservation software allows you to do all that electronically as well.

Month:

Date	Sun	Mon	Tues	Wed	Thu	Fri	Sat
#1. Blue Room							
Guest							
Arr. Time							
Deposit							
Notes							
#2. Red Room							
Guest							
Arr. Time							
Deposit							
Notes							
#3. Green Room							
Guest							
Arr. Time							
Deposit							
Notes							
#4. Maple Suite							
Guest							
Arr. Time							
Deposit							
Notes							
#5. Elm Suite							
Guest							
Arr. Time							
Deposit							
Notes							
#6. Chestnut Room							
Guest							
Arr. Time							
Deposit							
Notes							

After the guest's stay, file the reservation cards or forms alphabetically or store them in your online database. This gives you a handy guest list for newsletter mailings and special promotions. If you are really organized, you might record pertinent details about the guest so that you can more easily remember their likes and dislikes when they return. When a returning guest whom you noted "especially liked the hazelnut soufflé" is served it again with a comment like "I hope you enjoy this as much the second time," the impression you leave is invaluable. No hotel can do that.

A system that includes sections for gift certificates, postponements, and your "A" list (yes, you will find yourself rating your guests) is also useful.

Care is the hallmark of the innkeeper; keeping detailed guest records on paper or electronically is but another example of that care. You should think enough of your guests to try to remember them. It takes effort, but that effort is appreciated.

HOUSEKEEPING AND MAINTENANCE

You are not only running an inn, but you are also managing a large property that needs regular upkeep. Guests cause wear and tear on your house (though not as much as a full-time live-in family), but they don't expect the wear and tear to show. Standards are higher for an inn than for a private home. At home, guests live with half-used soap and toilet paper and frayed towels, but they expect better from an inn.

Here's a look at what your home can expect from temporary residents: nicks and scrapes from large suitcases bumping against walls and furniture, stopped-up toilets, window shades knocked askew, scratched and worn floors and carpets from considerable traffic in entrance areas and public areas, worn mattresses (some of your guests will be quite large), chipped china, broken glasses, stained napkins and bedsheets. Your linens will also wear out surprisingly quickly. Because of frequent washing, towels may last no more than four months, no matter how good the quality. Oddly enough, older sheets can feel really comfortable, so they will last longer than towels.

Carol Ringoot, former innkeeper at the Thomas Shepherd Inn in Shepherdstown, West Virginia, says that she was always astonished at how many lightbulbs she needed. You will be, too; you're keeping more lights on longer for the safety and comfort of your guests. And you will use lots of toilet paper—we have no idea what guests do with it all!

You should have a basic complement of tools and hardware—screwdrivers and extra screws, hammer, nails, pliers, furniture glue, plumber's wrench, and so on. They should be easy to find and kept in working order. Take care of small items as you go. Towel bars, which come loose as people yank towels off, need to be tightened; luggage racks and chairs often need regluing. Following are some suggestions of routine maintenance and preventative maintenance to give your equipment and furniture a longer life:

• Get maintenance contracts on major appliances and house components. "An in-home contract for your computer is a must, because it's too hard to leave the inn," advises Felipe Gaston of the Evans House B&B Inn in Sausalito, California.

• Use mattress covers on all mattresses, and pillow ticks or covers on the pillows.

• Put "egg-crate" foam pads between mattresses and box springs.

• Turn and flip the mattresses regularly (at least every quarter, unless you have the new no-turn mattresses) and vacuum them.

• Set up a painting schedule. For example, paint one-quarter of the interior and exterior each year, so that by the end of four years you've redone the entire house.

• Replace filters on air conditioners and furnaces at least every other month.

• Have wood-burning chimneys swept each season.

• Clean out the gutters once or twice a year.

Get in the habit of doing maintenance fairly regularly. We do maintenance seasonally, anticipating what needs to be done by several weeks. Most innkeepers learn this the hard way—when snow arrives is not the time to be outside putting up storm windows. As with everything else, scheduling is every-thing. You have to think ahead.

Even if the house is empty, you need to keep on top of the housekeeping. A rotating schedule of cleaning is a good idea. Freshen the rooms between guests, and do a good cleaning weekly, at the least. Always change towels every day and sheets every other day (some innkeepers wait until the third day, but we think that is too long).

Train your staff to make the beds the way you want them made. This is not as simple as you might think. The usual order: fitted bottom sheet, top sheet, blanket, third sheet (if you wish to do triple sheeting to save your blanket), bedspread or duvet. Pillows may be covered by the spread or put in shams. Extra pillows can be put on the bed or removed to a closet shelf. You don't want the bed made army-style, with everything tucked in tightly. Hospital corners are best.

It's all the little things together that make a room special: window shades even, fringes on oriental rugs straight, towels neatly arranged on the towel bars, pillows plumped, spreads even, dust ruffles neatly pleated.

AMENITIES

Amenities are part and parcel of inn-going. A true amenity goes beyond what is expected of any good room. Amenities do not include mirrors in the bathrooms, good reading lights, com-fortable chairs, comfortable beds, blankets, closets, and a sitting room for guests. You ought to have these things, and you should not consider them amenities.

Amenities are surprises: nice soaps, unusually large and fluffy towels, bathrobes, afternoon tea, fresh flowers, fresh fruit, games in the public sitting room, books and magazines, and so on. Guests have come to expect some little amenities—the more expensive the inn, the more they expect them—and innkeep-ers delight in providing them. Here are the amenities provided by some innkeepers:

Josh and Jeanine Rudolph of 1814 House, Doylestown, Penn-sylvania: Free high-speed Internet access, two telephone lines per room, early-morning coffee, free upgrades during slower time periods, free morning newspaper, two-person whirlpool baths, and CD/DVD players in every room.

Deb and Gary Leitner of Hillside Farm, Lancaster County, Pennsylvania: Smoke-free rooms; first-floor rooms for the handicapped; soap, shampoo, and other bath products in the bathrooms; large, fluffy towels; extra blankets in the rooms; bathrobes in closets of rooms with shared baths; clocks in each room; separate thermostats for each room; ceiling fans in each room; magazines and books in each room; games, puzzles, and TV in the common area; rocking chairs on the porch; cold spring water in each room; refrigerator for guest use; special items for anniversary, birthday, or honeymoon guests.

Mae McQuade of Split-Pine Farmhouse, Pine Grove Mills, Pennsylvania: Hampers of sodas and buckets of ice in the upstairs hallways; lovely glasses on the servers; cordials and small glasses in each room; special soaps; tea or coffee for weary travelers; potpourri and flowers from the garden.

Richard Carlson of Ballastone Inn, Savannah: Full-service bar, courtyard, elevators, turndown service, free off-street parking, public spaces, fireplaces, whirlpool baths.

Guests are more likely to pay extra for private in-room amenities, such as whirlpool baths, fireplaces, views, balconies, and oversize beds, than they are for public amenities like acreage, walking trails, or extra sitting rooms. This means that offering more private amenities can yield greater income. Many successful innkeepers have invested in their businesses by upgrading and adding in-room luxury amenities, and then raising their rates accordingly. After the payoff of the capital expenditure, the higher marginal room charge is all profit.

A few words of caution about fireplaces, hot tubs, and whirlpool baths: These can be dangerous items for guests or for your house. Make sure that they are not set up dangerously and that your guests know how to use them. Gas fireplaces with timers are easier to deal with and safer than wood-burning ones, guests don't have to get out of bed to feed them, and they don't leave an odor behind. If you deal with wood-burning fireplaces much, you'll quickly understand why our ancestors closed them up and went to central heating. Be very careful about shared hot tubs. Make the rules clear: no pregnant women or unsupervised young children. Pregnant women should not use whirlpool baths either. Hyperthermia can kill. Hot tubs are also difficult to keep clean, and soap scum can transfer diseases. For these reasons, we do not recommend these appliances be installed.

Bar service, too, can cause liability problems. If you want to serve drinks, make sure your insurance covers host liquor liability issues. Fewer guests are drinking heavily these days, and you can easily get by without serving liquor, although home-made liqueurs can be a nice touch. Some of your guests may be recovering alcoholics; do not be insistent about offering alcohol, because you may be tempting a guest unkindly. Also, more states have zero-tolerance laws today when it comes to drinking and driving. Many guests ask if we are within walking distance of downtown—that often means they want to have a few glasses of wine with dinner without having to drive.

Afternoon tea or refreshments are increasingly becoming an expected amenity at inns. In any season, an appropriate nonalcoholic beverage is appreciated: iced tea with mint from your garden in summer, hot apple cider with a cinnamon stick in winter. Guests appreciate being offered something late in the afternoon, after a long day of driving or sightseeing.

Offering food is a time-honored way of saying, "Welcome," and we recommend it. As Dinie says, low-cost, simple, yet thoughtful amenities, such as a plate of home-baked cookies or a bowl of fruit in the common room, are often the most appreciated. If you serve a more elaborate tea, most innkeepers recommend that you set the time with guests. That way you won't be fixing tea or washing glasses all day long. And getting all the guests together at once with a cup or glass helps lubricate the social interaction that characterizes inns at their best.

Turndown service is a matter of controversy. Owen doesn't feel comfortable doing it; he considers it to be an invasion of a guest's privacy. And as a business traveler on the road, Ripley

always found it silly to see the spread turned back and a chocolate on the pillow. Why chocolate at that time of the night?
Don't do turndown service—or any other amenity—if you think
it's silly. It won't be *you* and therefore will violate the principles
of good innkeeping.

On the other hand, if you think turndown service adds a special touch, by all means do it, and put a mint or a flower or an
embroidered take-home gift on the pillow. This is a labor-
intensive amenity, but it offers you a chance to straighten the
room and put in fresh towels, which are much appreciated. If
you don't do the service, then you need to supply extra towels
in the room or in some convenient place. Lesley Hubbard of
the Victoria and Albert Inn in Abingdon, Virginia, puts huge
baskets of fluffy towels in her shared baths—a beautiful and
thoughtful touch. There must be twenty towels in each of those
baskets. Keep in mind, too, that if you want to go for AAA four-
diamond status, offering turndown service is one of the things
expected. You don't actually have to do it unless the guest asks,
but you do have to offer it.

Some amenities depend on the area. Ski lockers or bicycles
are useful at some inns. Others offer health club, golfing, or
swimming privileges at nearby resorts or country clubs.
Anything that extends what your inn offers can be considered
an amenity. Your guests will say that you are a thoughtful, caring host who goes far beyond what a hotel or motel would do.

One of the most important amenities you can provide is to
share what you know about your area, to offer your out-of-town
guests an insider's perspective. If you are a good tour guide, you
can make sure your guests have a good time. Use this as a way
to suggest to your guests that there is so much more to do in
your area than they can hope to cover in one visit. This will
encourage them to return.

Historic inns offer tours of the house. Telling stories about its
history or decorations often delights guests. Of course, there are
some guests who say, "Skip the tour; just show me my room."

Is a guest telephone an amenity? Less so than it used to be,
since the advent of cell phones. An extra phone with a separate number (so that the inn's line isn't kept busy) is not a major

expense. If you do not designate a long-distance carrier, guests can use their credit cards or call collect. That way you won't have to worry about someone putting large charges on your bill.

Modern technology now makes providing in-room Internet access and in-room telephones relatively easy. If you have a second number, you can buy a base station that plugs into your electrical wiring and a satellite plug that can be put in any room in the house, creating a telephone jack there. The prevalence of cellular telephones has not made the need for in-room telephones obsolete: traditional telephone instruments with an extra jack for a laptop to plug into is a very popular and appreciated amenity.

The latest communications amenity is the wireless access point (WAP). If you have high-speed Internet access, such as DSL or a cable modem, it's easy and inexpensive to add a wireless router that will let your guests have access with their laptops from anywhere in your inn. It also allows you to add another computer to your network easily if you want to do that.

Although guests at inns are not couch-potato types, and in-room TVs are not expected amenities in all parts of North America, some guests feel the need to stay connected to world news even while on a short getaway, especially since September 11. Others like to watch the Weather Channel or other twenty-four-seven channels. TV sets with built-in VCRs or DVDs are fairly inexpensive, and running cable to the rooms is not difficult. Providing a videotape or DVD library for your guests is a much-appreciated amenity.

You really must have a TV in the public room, at least, because television has become a sort of shared public space of its own. Wives often go out shopping, leaving their husbands to enjoy a football game. Sometimes, if you arrange this unobtrusively, both halves of the couple will thank you. (In order not to be accused of sexism, we'll acknowledge the existence of football-watching wives and shopping husbands, though they are not in the majority.) Anyway, try to accommodate everyone.

Special soaps and other bathroom amenities are becoming clichés, as even low-end hotels offer them. You can do a little extra advertising if you put your inn's logo and phone number on them. Guests often like to buy a box of soaps to take home; some inns pay for their soaps with these sales. You might consider adding a few of the following items to the usual soap and shampoo found in guest bathrooms: glycerine soap for those with sensitive skin, shoe mitts (these will discourage guests from using your washcloths to polish shoes), shower caps, a mending kit, hand lotion, bubble bath, cologne, or after-shave lotion. You might also want to put in a small supply of extra toothbrushes and toothpaste, disposable razors, shaving cream, and any other item that guests might have forgotten. Calls for these are not frequent, but having them on hand shows that you are especially thoughtful. Another one useful bathroom amenity is makeup removal cloths. After you've had to relegate several nice white washcloths or pillowcases to the rag bag because of mascara, you'll see the value in this. If you do one-of-a-kind towel sets, makeup stains can become a source of real irritation—and expense.

Fresh flowers in rooms or the common area show thoughtfulness to your guests, but they are, in many areas, very expensive—prohibitively so in certain seasons. Green plants are nice and last longer, but they require watering, which is easy to forget in the haste of changing rooms from one guest to another.

In general, balance your rates, costs, and occupancy to decide how far you will go with amenities. The costs can mount quickly. You could easily spend $40 to $50 per guest room on amenities if you went whole hog. If your rates are high enough, they may justify (or require) that expense. But don't start out with more than you can easily manage, because it can be difficult to subtract amenities.

BOOKKEEPING

You must keep good records, if for no other reason than tax purposes. If you really hate bookkeeping—and we know very few people who like it—then make it as easy on yourself as possible. Put all your bills in one place. Record the amounts and descriptions of all payments in your online or paper checkbook. Record all receipts from your guests. Then each quarter, give everything to your bookkeeper or accountant. Quicken and Quick Books software can do all this for you. Many states and localities require monthly payment of taxes you have collected; don't miss the deadlines or you will regret it.

Note that we said to record *all* receipts from your guests. We know that some restaurants and inns pocket cash receipts without recording them so as to avoid paying sales and income taxes. Do not do this! Not only is it dishonest (hiding income = jail time), but it will also work to your disadvantage in the long run.

Suppose, about six years down the road, you are doing a good business—perhaps 50 percent occupancy—and have been pocketing a few thousand in cash a month without recording it. You decide to sell your thriving business, but your books show you grossing about $10,000 less than you really are. The value of your business is usually figured as a multiple of gross receipts. As a result, your selling price may be tens of thousands of dollars less than your inn's actual value, because you cannot prove you took in that money. Worse, if you tell the potential buyer that you have been skimming the profits, that buyer is going to wonder about your honesty in other areas.

Paper Systems

Although you don't want to be an accountant, you will probably be taking in the receipts and paying the bills yourself. There are lots of ways of doing this, but the best paper accounting system is a "one-write" pegboard.

If you've never used one, here's how it works: Checks are arranged in a layered series, with carbon strips under the payee line. Thus, when you write a check, the same information goes directly onto your bookkeeping page underneath. When you get to the bottom of the page, you total the columns and carry the figure over to the next page. The same is true of receipts.

One-write systems are widely available at office supply stores, from your bank or accountant, or through the Professional Association of Innkeepers International, if you join. The KISS (Keep It Simple Stupid) principle is the recommended way to go initially.

The Computer in the Inn

Computers are a love-hate thing. Here you are hearing from innkeepers on both sides: Carl hates them; Ripley loves them (and hates fixing them). Small inns can't make really efficient use of computers unless one of the partners is already reasonably computer literate.

They are, however, becoming essential, not just for bookkeeping, but also for communications. The Internet has changed everything, and if you cannot handle e-mail and the browser, you are going to miss a huge amount of business. Also, if you want to do your own e-marketing, bookkeeping, and accounting to save some money, the computer is indispensable. Computers perform dozens of tasks, freeing much of your time for the more personal aspects of innkeeping. They can also help keep your inn afloat by giving you early warning of problems.

Because there are so many different tasks you can use the computer for, innkeepers need several programs to do them: a database for guest lists, a word-processing program, an accounting program for bookkeeping, and perhaps a spreadsheet, if you want to do pretty pictures of your occupancy rate.

Now there are excellent guest reservation systems— Rezovation is perhaps the best known and most widely used. This and similar programs give you many useful reports, as well as keeping track of reservations, allowing you to print letters or send e-mail responses and manage the guest list. They are essentially databases. They also connect directly to your online reservations or availability system to update them.

Online availability systems are becoming essential. Many are free, but the paid ones have better features, and some are both availability systems and online booking systems. Some of them are Availability Online, EU Bookings, InnRes, Inntopia, Net Bookings, and Webervations. You can find all of them, and probably more, on the Internet.

One useful feature of some of the availability systems is that they allow you to check availability of your own group, should you choose to share the information. In Asheville, for example, we use InnRes for the Asheville Bed and Breakfast Association.

We can see all the available rooms for all of the inns in the group and, if necessary, can direct guests to another inn with the assurance that there is a room available there.

Some innkeepers allow potential guests to see availability room by room. If you're interested in how that works, you're welcome to check the availability of rooms at www.biltmore villageinn.com. The current owner of the 1900 Inn on Montford, Lynn Carlson, does not choose to do that. Her argument is that if guests don't see that you have something available, you might be able to talk them into a higher-rate room than they had intended, whereas if they can see what's available room-by-room and the rate, they might never call. It's a sound argument, and you have to decide which approach is best for you.

Don't become overwhelmed trying to do everything yourself. Use your computer for communicating with guests, property management, and accounting, and if necessary, subcontract certain functions to a computer service: word processing, guest record files, and mass mailings, when your list gets large enough. You can make good use of a machine that keeps daily records with a few keystrokes instead of piling up receipts until you need to pay an accountant to straighten them out.

A notebook computer or personal digital assistant (PDA) is portable and allows you to keep the business going while you're away from the inn for a few days. Replying to e-mail, checking your online reservations, and doing online banking can all be performed on your wireless PDA or notebook computer. Then they can synchronize with your base computer on your return.

A FEW OTHER WAYS TO MAKE MONEY

Besides a restaurant—and there are some doubts that these are real moneymakers—there are a few ways to bring additional money into the inn.

Many innkeepers left other careers in order to do what they liked with their time, but all those hard-learned skills need not go to waste. Many of us liked our earlier careers (but not the nine-to-five part), so why leave them behind entirely?

Take advantage of your previous profession. Try consulting or some other extension of what you used to do. If you wish, you can run both income and expenses through your inn; because you're an employee, all the money you make goes to the inn, and all your expenses are covered. This can be an efficient use of your time if you can bring in more money through your sideline than you would pay someone else to do some chore around the inn that you would otherwise do yourself.

Another useful way to bring in money is to have a shop in or attached to the inn. Small items, from soaps to antiques to travel books, can net enough to make it worth doing. Of course, you have to be a capable buyer. You can also work out arrangements with local craftspeople, farmers, and so on to stock parts of your shop on consignment. You can include items that you make or bake yourself; cookies go over nicely, as do homemade breads and jams. Spend a little time at a local craft fair, and you'll quickly see what is available.

Many of your guests will look for souvenirs; postcards and sketches (framed or not) of the inn are good to have. Fluffy bathrobes, polo shirts, and ceramic plates or mugs with your inn logo are also popular gift shop items. The list can go on and on. Some towns have limits on this, however; Asheville specifically prohibits gift shops in bed-and-breakfast inns.

Most successful shopkeepers say that in order to work, the shop has to have a clearly marked place of its own, even if it is just a corner cupboard or glass-enclosed curio cabinet. Then you need to notify your guests (and others) that it is available, through your website, brochure, or guest letter, or in your opening spiel.

Another strong trend for inns is offering spa services—even a full service spa in a separate building. Other innkeepers earn extra income by marking up add-on services offered at their inn. You may be able to negotiate a wholesale rate from a masseuse, florist, or chocolatier in exchange for being your exclusive supplier. Then charge your guest retail, pocketing the 20 percent or so margin. Yet other innkeepers make some extra money by offering packages. And guests are very interested in packages these days.

One thing we do not approve of is price tags on all the fur-nishings. Giving guests the impression that they are staying in the middle of a furniture sales floor is not conducive to the friendly, homey atmosphere you are trying to create.

EMPLOYEES

When you add employees—and if your inn has more than four rooms, you'll need to in order to avoid burnout—you can count on having problems. Not all of them are serious problems, but having employees will require more of your time and attention. That means other aspects of your inn will get less. Since your primary job is providing personal service, any diversion is a problem.

Owners who are not prepared for this step can do irrepara-ble harm to their inns. They tend to interfere constantly in the work of those they hire. They refuse to delegate responsibility as well as tasks. And they never believe anyone else can do it as well as they do. With some of the people you hire, that may be true. Few chambermaids will care as you do about the cleanli-ness of rooms. Few of them will work as quickly as you do. If you find one who does, hold on to that treasure.

Rather than hiring chambermaids, you might try using a pro-fessional cleaning service. You have to be prepared to step in if the service doesn't show, but you can more easily say to the owner that a certain worker just isn't right for your inn. Such services don't exist for assistant innkeepers and inn-sitters, however, so you'll probably have to deal with employees anyway.

Very little in handling employees is free of legal constraints. Because governments often measure the size and success of your company by the number of people you hire, and because most of their taxes come from workers with jobs, all government entities will be deeply interested whenever you hire.

When you do hire, especially for positions that require some thought, you should write job descriptions. That's a service both to you and to your potential employees. Your job descrip-tions can be centered on responsibilities, specific duties, or both. They should be precise enough that anyone with reasonable qualifications can look at the description and know fairly well what needs to be done. Don't be too restrictive in your descriptions; you don't want to overmanage your employees or you'll kill initiative.

If you're hiring an assistant innkeeper, initiative is important. You have to make clear from the start, however, that the inn is yours, and that everything must be done in keeping with the personality you have created for it. If you let a strong-willed assistant impose her own taste or methods where you prefer yours, you will have added a headache rather than a helper.

Working with People

A good boss is hard to find. It isn't that most bosses want to be difficult; it's that they are uncomfortable, they don't know how to be better, or they think they're good when they really aren't. And besides, most of us left the corporate world to get away from bosses.

Remember how it used to be, and do your best to be a good boss. If you aren't, your associates won't work well or together, and you, your employees, and your guests will all end up unhappy. Guests regard everyone who works in the inn as being there for them. When a guest wants ice, she'll ask the chambermaid, and it won't do to have the request greeted with "That ain't my job," "I dunno," or "Huh?" Train all your employees to understand that the guests come first—within the limits of the house rules.

Training is constant. It has to be, because you will learn something new nearly every day that you're an inn owner, and as you learn new things, you have to pass them on to your staff.

You need to see and talk to your employees often. If you don't, they'll think something is wrong and wonder what they've done. In fact, any sudden change in your usual behavior is liable to set off speculation. You also need to explain, reexplain, and reinforce the policies and procedures you have established for your guests' happiness. Depending on the size of your operation, you may want to have formal meetings once a week.

If you have only a few employees, a brief chat in the kitchen at the start of the workday may suffice.

If you have a partner, do not disagree with one another in front of employees. If one of you says something the other dislikes, bring it up in private, come to an agreement, and follow through with what you agreed on.

If you have a particular way you want things done by the chambermaids, explain first, then check after the first few times the work is done. You should be quick to praise and equally quick to point out errors. But don't micromanage; a white-glove inspection every time a room is cleaned will probably lose you a lot of workers.

Try to make your employees into partners of sorts (they might be someday, if you sell the place to them over time). Encourage them to solve problems with guests, and give them the same right to make mistakes as you gave yourself. You should expect good work from them, and you should expect them to serve your guests well. But remember, you are the final authority. If a room isn't properly cleaned, you're going to hear about it. If a new assistant innkeeper overbooks, you're going to have to pay to put the guests somewhere else.

Some Legal Considerations

Governments take an interest in your relationships with your employees. Chances are you'll never hear from them, but you might. The best thing you can do for your business is to know where problem areas are and make sure you're operating properly in those areas.

You must give every applicant the same chance to be hired. You may not give different exams or interview questions to different candidates. In fact, you would be wise not to use an employment test at all, since so many are considered discriminatory. All candidates must be judged on the same grounds. Do not discriminate against any candidate on the grounds of sex, race, religion, national origin, age, disability, or sexual preference. If you disappoint a candidate and he or she is able to show a pattern of discrimination in hiring, you may find yourself the object of an Equal Employment Opportunity Commission inquiry. The same cautions apply to promotions and compensation.

In an interview or job application form, you will be in trouble if you ask about things such as a candidate's age or marital status; those questions could be discriminatory. You can't ask about credit ratings or arrest records. You can ask about criminal convictions, although you have to be careful then that you ask every candidate the question. You can't require high school graduation unless that is clearly necessary for someone to do the job.

If someone is disabled in some obvious way, you may not discriminate just because you think they can't do the job. For example, if a person is confined to a wheelchair, you may not assume that he or she can't clean rooms (you would be wrong). Further, someone in a wheelchair might make an excellent desk clerk. You *can* legitimately say that he or she is not going to be able to clean rooms in your inn because you have two floors and no elevator. Think about what the job requires and let that, not their disabilities, guide you.

Background checks can also get you into trouble if you use them to find out about matters not included on an application form. You should check those things that the candidate does put down. A simple phone call to a high school or college to check on graduation will tell you at least that you have an honest person.

Because employers can be sued if they give an unfavorable recommendation of a former employee, you may have a great deal of trouble getting an honest evaluation. Some companies now prohibit managers from giving out any information about a former employee, even the very best ones, except that the person did work for the company and was paid at a certain level. You might end up talking to someone who will tell you the truth anyway, but don't count on it. For these reasons, recommendation letters and references are growing increasingly worthless.

You need to make sure that you are not hiring an illegal alien. Regulations in this area are subject to change. To find out the latest on hiring questions related to immigration law, check the Immigration and Naturalization Service website at uscis.gov/graphics/index.htm.

Wage scales have to be fair and cannot be below the minimum wage, although there are some exceptions for certain occupations and age groups. This area, too, changes fairly often. For the latest, see the Department of Labor website at www.dol.gov/.

Benefits are an exceptionally tough area. You have to pay unemployment tax, Social Security tax (7.5 percent of your employee's net salary, at this writing), and your state's worker's compensation insurance. But you may wish to offer other benefits. If you can afford to, it's an excellent idea, as it helps attract better help. The first benefit offered is usually paid vacation, followed by health benefits, and then by retirement programs. But usually only large operations with steady, growing business can manage this.

Many federal laws and regulations do not apply to very small companies (usually those with less than ten employees), but you can't count on that. State laws, often more restrictive, regulate employee treatment in companies with as few as three employees.

If all fails and you make a bad hire, you need to correct the error as soon as possible. Document each instance of unacceptable performance, including the date, a description of incident, and the reason. Vague explanations such as "She doesn't get along with others" won't hold up as grounds for firing.

Observing these legal niceties is important. Unfair discharge or hiring suits can drain your company and you. And once you are involved in a lawsuit, nothing except consistently good records and practices will help you.

INSURANCE

You need to have adequate commercial property and liability coverage for your business; a homeowner's policy is not sufficient to protect an inn. Accidents happen, and we live in a litigious nation. You need to have at least a $1 million liability policy and appropriate loss coverage in case of fire or other disaster.

This is more than just a business; usually all your furnishings and home equity are involved as well. You may obtain a separate tenant's policy to cover your personal belongings, although many newer policies cover them along with those of the inn. A number of ancillary policies and riders also can be tailored to your particular situation.

Since the September 11, 2001, terrorist attack, all insurance premiums have risen dramatically. After debt service and taxes, your insurance premium will often be tied with utilities for the third-highest fixed expense.

Coverage can vary greatly among underwriters, so research your options carefully before choosing a policy, and recheck annually before renewal time. You need to find a good agent who understands inns; most agents do not. Many companies that are good for auto insurance will not insure inns. Litigiousness among guests has risen recently, and some underwriters are dropping out of the business. Find a good local insurance agent who will research possible underwriters and keep you informed of rate changes.

9

Don't Forget the Guests

"WHAT A GREAT JOB! A GUEST PAYS TO STAY IN MY
HOME, GIVES ME A LITTLE GIFT BEFORE DEPARTING, AND
THEN SENDS ME A HANDWRITTEN THANK-YOU CARD
FOR MY HOSPITALITY!"

—Richard Butkus

All innkeepers will agree that the most fun—and the most
trials—of this business involve guests. But that's as it should
be, isn't it? After all, you became an innkeeper so that you could
serve your guests.

You already have in mind who those guests will be, and you
have created your inn for them. Your success as an innkeeper
depends on what they think of you. That means you have to
know (or learn) how to anticipate needs and how to do exactly
what the guest expects—even before the guest expects it.

On the one hand, you'll find that guests can be demanding,
even without intending to be. On the other, you'll find that they
can be surprisingly tolerant, willing to put up with almost anything to make you feel better. Some guests will be so obnoxious
you never want to see them again; others you will want to keep
for friends.

But you're also expecting them to pay. And they're expecting
you to serve them. A delicate relationship, that.

The most important thing to realize is that 99 percent of your guests will be great and will make everything you do worthwhile. You'll remember every one of the others, but that's probably because there are so few clinkers.

"Seacrest Manor is like heaven. Booked for one night and stayed seven." What prompts a guest to write such a comment? According to innkeeper Leighton Saville, "We have offered a consistently high level of service to our houseguests each and every day since opening." Business partner Dwight Mac-Cormack says: "We don't allow wedding parties at our inn, even though we have the facilities, because of the noise and other factors. We have turned away midweek and off-season business because of this rule, but we feel we must stick to our guns in order to be fair to our clientele who want peace and quiet." They both agree that treating their inn guests with the same respect and attention they would give a family friend in their own home is the most effective way to build strong repeat business.

You need to go the extra mile with your guests, not only because you like to or because they are paying you, but also because they are two of the three major sources of additional business for you: repeat visits and referrals.

Being a host, especially a paid host, is not an easy job. Yes, your inn is your stage, but you don't belong at the center of it all the time. The best host is unobtrusive—there when your guests want you, but not if they don't. As Dinie says, "accessible but not overbearing nor intrusive."

This is a hard lesson for most of us. One of the very best things about innkeeping is realizing that we can tell all our tired stories over and over again. Guests are new victims! If your stories are good, then perhaps you should be on center stage. On the other hand, most guests are too polite to tell you that they've had enough of you. You have to learn to be quiet without being asked.

As you set your policies, keep in mind that you must balance your business needs with your guests' needs. That requires flexibility in delicate situations. Ask yourself whether it is possible to create a win-win outcome when a guest is unhappy.

You also have to balance the needs of your various guests. Sometimes the demands of one will cause you to be less hospitable to the others. There are ways to deal with most of these situations, but something new always seems to come up. One of the most frequent comments innkeepers make is "You'd think after seven (or three or ten) years in this business, you would have seen everything. But guests will always surprise you."

We obviously can't tell you everything about dealing with guests, but we can give you some hints for how to handle situations guaranteed to come up. Some problems can be handled by your established policies, but many solutions depend on your style and your ability to think on your feet. Innkeepers have to learn to roll with the punches. Without flexibility, these situations will surely drive you mad.

AT THE FRONT DOOR

Your welcome sets the whole tone for a guest's visit. It's possible to recover from a disastrous greeting, but it takes more work than doing it right from the start.

Michael Barrier, a colleague, writer about inns, and frequent inn-goer, says, "Because an inn is so much more homelike than a hotel, guests are much more likely to feel as if they are intruding if the innkeeper's greeting is not warm."

We ought not to have to say this, but we will: Your inn is a public accommodation by law. You cannot ignore federal and state civil rights laws protecting citizens from discrimination because of age, race, sexual orientation, creed, or national origin. If you have any personal prejudices, it is illegal to bring them into your business. If someone whom you have a prejudice against comes to your door, you owe them the same warm welcome any other guest would get. If you cannot do this, find another business.

Sometimes innkeepers have trouble maintaining warmth at greeting—especially if they've just seen the arriving guest drive over a newly planted flowerbed. Or if the first words out of a guest's mouth are, "Your beds had better be comfortable, because I have a bad back." You have to bite your tongue to keep from answering, "Actually, it's not your back that's bad, it's your attitude."

The best way to greet your guests is to smile, say, "Welcome to the inn," and tell them your name and who you are. Many are first-timers and really don't know quite what to expect. Most people are used to being able to push open the lobby door of a motel or hotel. They are not accustomed to finding the door locked (as a B&B most often is) and having to ring a bell to enter. They're also not accustomed to being greeted by the owner and may expect a clerk (alas, some travelers do not treat clerks as well as they would an owner).

Former innkeeper Darlene McNeill says that one of the highest compliments that an innkeeper can give is not to look harried or pressured when the guest arrives. She may have a scrub brush behind the door, but in front of the door she has a smile. Annette King advises: "If you look sloppy, with dirty sneakers and mussed hair, then you'll likely get sloppy guests. They may think they have permission to be careless with your home."

Ripley and Owen tend to dress quite casually when guests arrive. Their reasoning is that the house is so formal that they need a few touches to tone down the formality and make it feel more homey. That's their way. This brings us back to the point that innkeeper and inn together create the ambience. You can't have one without the other.

Ripley remembers with pleasure a couple of his first guests (who subsequently returned every year) who drove up in a Jaguar. He was riding Boydville's brand new tractor-mower, wearing jeans and a lumberjack shirt. Without thinking, he hopped off the mower, grabbed up their luggage and took it into the house, invited them to sign the register, and then showed them to their room, whereupon the gentleman tried to tip him $2. The guest was later surprised to see the person he thought was the yard man serving breakfast. At least it was a warm greeting.

If your building lends itself to a tour, by all means do one when the guests arrive. They don't always want one, and if not, don't force it. But most guests do. Even if you don't have a distinctive or historic building, you should show guests where the common room is and tell them any other little facts they should know, like where breakfast is served and when, where the guest pantry is, where the telephone or the TV set or hot tub is, and where they should or should not walk.

Some inns handle these details by putting "room letters" in the rooms. The Inn at Twin Linden gives guests a chatty room letter that tells them useful bits of information such as where to get ice, which doors to use, where the hot tub is (and who should not use it), and so on. Having these details in writing is often more effective; people do forget, especially when they are trying to take in so much.

One important piece of information that you should give every guest on arrival is how to find you should that be necessary. Emergencies do occur. If you aren't resident and don't have a resident manager, then you should be quickly available by telephone. If you are resident, let guests know what door to knock on if they can't seem to get any hot water, would like to borrow an ironing board, or have a bottle of wine to chill. Make it easy for guests to find you if they need to.

Also make clear to guests how you do breakfast. This is not standard from inn to inn, and should not be. Some inns offer continental breakfasts whenever the guests like; others have guests sign up for different serving times; still others serve all guests at the same time. The Wedgwood also offers the option of a breakfast tray in the guestroom or alfresco. Most serve the same thing to all guests, but some present menus.

All innkeepers we've spoken to will accommodate special dietary needs with advance notification. If you plan to serve the same menu to all guests, you need to find out if any guests have food allergies or restrictions. And there are more and more special dietary requirements, from low fat to low carb to wheat-free, and on and on. You may not be able to please everyone (wheat and dairy allergies are especially difficult to accommodate at breakfast), but you should be able to offer some simple alternatives. A little trick many of us use: When serving an egg dish, keep the breakfast meat on the side and not mixed with the eggs. This allows a kosher or vegetarian guest to still eat your egg dish. In any case, make sure your guests know how breakfast is done. It is, after all, a major component of a B&B.

Finally, before your guests move off to their rooms, you need to make the kinds of offers that will show them you are thinking of them: Do they need a dinner reservation? Would they like any information about what to do in the area? Do they need directions anywhere? Would they like some tea or lemonade and cookies? Nancie and Lee Cabana, formerly of Brookview Manor Inn, offered newly arrived guests their own copies of a map of the hiking trail that leads to a nearby waterfall. Most inns provide menus of area restaurants, brochures to attractions and shopping, and sometimes even tickets to special events.

HANDLING GROUPS

Inns are becoming popular places for—and are promoting themselves as—locations for weddings, parties, small business meetings, reunions, and retreats. Of these, weddings are the most trying. In general, the more people, the more problems. If you want to take on these functions, by all means do so, but be aware of what you're getting into.

Special events can be a good source of income for inns, but they require a great deal more thought than you would imagine. They are also very labor intensive. Many people think they know how to throw a party or run a meeting, but few really do.

Weddings and Parties

Why are weddings the worst? Much of it has to do with the stress inherent in weddings. It is (or is supposed to be) a once-in-a-lifetime event in the lives of two people, and the best weddings seem to be the ones completely planned by the people being married. But tradition dictates that the bride's mother is the party giver, the bride's father pays the bills and stays out of the way, and the groom's parents have very little to do but show up. Brides and grooms, unless they are very strong-willed, are often left aside.

The traditional wedding is often the bride's mother's opportunity to pay back every social obligation she has and to show that she can throw a great party. She rarely knows much about the groom's family or friends, and often not much more about her daughter's friends. The bride's father is usually unseen and unheard from, except when he is complaining about the mounting cost.

Into this situation steps the innkeeper, eager to get the business and to please. These two impulses, generous and well meant though they may be, often work against the best interests of the inn. If the bride's parents pay for all the rooms to put up the bride's party, then you have a house full of nonpaying guests. This, we assure you, is not good. Nonpaying guests will often take advantage of your hospitality, and you will end up disliking them. They are there to party, not necessarily to experience your inn, and by golly they will party.

The bride's mother will try to get you to lower the cost or throw in little extras. If you give in too easily to this kind of pressure, you will end up hating the party, the people, and the inn. This is true to some degree of all gatherings, but more so of weddings. In order to avoid difficulties, you must have a written contract that sets your rules firmly. Do not depart from them under any circumstances, even—especially—for your own friends and family.

We suggest these basic rules for innkeepers who want to host weddings or parties:

• Set a firm price for a specified time frame that you will be happy with. Quote an hourly rental rate for any time over the allotted period. This will give you incentive to put out whatever extra effort is called for.

• Establish a payment policy. We suggest making half due on the signing of an agreement and the remainder due the week before the event. If the money isn't in hand, cancel the event and keep the deposit. You may lose business, but you won't lose your shirt.

- List all services you will provide and their prices. Then stick to them. If you have estimated incorrectly and it costs you money, that's your tough luck. But if the party giver doesn't live up to the agreement, you have the deposit to fall back on.

- Add a service charge for outside services (flowers, catering, rentals) that you arrange. Your time is worth at least 10 percent. Smart party givers will let you make the arrangements. Smart suppliers will work hard, because you represent repeat business to them and they won't want to risk offending you by not doing a good job. Your one-time party giver may not get the same quality of service that you can get. Even having explained this to many brides' mothers, we have found that they often still opt to save the 10 percent by doing it themselves. They have usually been sorry. We have been tempted to refuse to do a wedding for which we do not make all the arrangements, but that seems a bit harsh. It may, however, be something you should consider. Many inns today will only work with preapproved vendors that they know and trust. The Wedgwood does, ever since an unknown caterer walked off with some of the inn's kitchen supplies.

- Insist on an adequate damage deposit, and make sure you check after the event for damage. Submit a written statement of damages and the amount you are withholding from the deposit to cover them.

All this may sound too tough for your traditional notion of innkeeping, but the situation demands it. Explaining your rules and having a contract signed at the beginning will be a lifesaver for you. If anything goes wrong from that point, it's your own fault. You'll learn quickly from your mistakes.

Business Meetings

You should not host meetings unless you are doing them for overnight guests. Unless your inn has a lot of public space, your regular guests will be disturbed, and you can't charge enough to make up for that annoyance. But business meetings are good midweek business, and one good meeting usually brings you more.

Business meetings have special requirements. Sometimes businesses have their own meeting planners to take care of these, but small ones depend on you to do that work.

You need to have a quiet place for the meeting, with good chairs, task lighting, and a table around which all the participants can sit. You can rent appropriate tables if you don't own them; include the rental in the price. If you want to do it right, provide notepads and pens or pencils (all with your inn's name printed on them).

Business meetings, if they go all day, generally start around 8:30 to 9 A.M., with coffee and possibly some pastries. There are usually two breaks, one at 10:30 A.M. and the other at 2:30 P.M., with lunch in between. You should serve coffee and soft drinks at the breaks. All these extras should be quoted in the price you negotiate. Do not just throw them in; you will be tending to your meeting guests all day long. That's bad business and is not expected.

Business meetings, though they may seem quiet, can drive you nuts. You have to take care of all those breaks and deal with the usual innkeeping requirements at the same time. There will often be requests for computer use, photocopying, faxing, telephone calls, and more. You may find yourself being used as a secretary. If you do it all cheerfully, you will probably get repeat business and referrals.

Retreats and Reunions
Retreats are popular with many groups, from religious and non-profit organizations to businesses. They combine the overnight stay with meetings and are therefore excellent business for inns—if you have enough rooms for them.

One advantage you offer to those planning retreats (especially business retreats) is that you can be an activities director for spouses who are brought along but have nothing to do. If you do a good job of entertaining the spouses, they will want to come back for vacations.

Retreats can try your patience. On more than one occasion, we have seen a group lose its maturity. For some reason, otherwise sober and dignified people can revert to teenage behavior when they are put together in an old house where everything is taken care of for them. It is therefore important to make the rules clear and be prepared to be (on occasion) a rather stern scoutmaster.

The same holds true for reunions, which can also include a contingent of thoroughly bored children. Families sometimes assume that they can use your kitchen or any other part of the inn they can reach. You need to make the limits clear.

DEALING WITH DIFFICULT GUESTS

We all hate to admit it, but there are indeed guests who try your patience. There are even a few (a very few) guests who make you wish you had never become an innkeeper. Because we are generally such optimists, we think this will never happen to us. We assume we're somehow going to be exempt from painful experiences with guests.

Not true, as everyone learns within the first few months. The traveling public is sensitive about costs, and with some rather unpleasant exposés out about the bad bargains some B&Bs are, guests occasionally arrive with chips on their shoulders. And we do sometimes make errors, which puts us in bad with guests, who then act pettishly.

As an innkeeper, you'll quickly develop a sense about guests. If a potential guest is inebriated or otherwise not legitimately suited for your establishment, your job is to say politely, "Sorry, no vacancy." You may perhaps make a referral to a more appropriate nearby motel. Many states have enacted an "Innkeepers Bill of Rights" to protect innkeepers from such guests and civil lawsuits that may arise as a result of their being denied accommodations.

Following are several types of difficult guests you're likely to encounter.

The Sourpusses

These guests arrive ready to complain and cannot be pleased. They will dislike something, and sometimes everything. And they will tell you.

Alas, sometimes they are right. If more than one guest complains about the same thing, then you'd better look into it. It may, in fact, be too cold in that room, or there may be a problem with the water pressure, or there may be too much noise from the next room. Sometimes complainers do you a favor by notifying you of a problem. Successful innkeepers do indeed learn from their guests' written or verbal comments.

Owen will never forget one doctor who walked in the door and demanded to know whether the inn had water beds (no). He said he had a bad back and couldn't sleep well without one. Owen—who was a furniture salesman and knows how to buy a good bed—smiled and said that he tried to have excellent beds because many guests have sensitive backs, but that he couldn't guarantee more than that. The doctor and his wife stayed, and he complained bitterly the next morning that the birds had awakened him. From that Owen assumed he had in fact slept well—but was never in a million years going to admit it.

The Critics

These guests compare you unfavorably with other inns. It doesn't make you happy to have someone tell you that the breakfast they had at Cozy Corners was so much nicer than yours. "They had such nice jams there," the critics will say. "You ought to find out what they have and get some." Do not dump jam on their heads. Smile and tell them you'll certainly inquire about it; letting guests feel superior is one of the pleasures you can afford them. And you might in fact find that the jam at Cozy Corners is rather special. We do tend to be thin-skinned about our places. There are lessons to be learned from other inns, and we don't get out to see them as much as we'd like.

The most tempting response to this kind of guest is "If you're so damn good at this, why don't you open an inn?" Think it, but don't say it. The business doesn't need an innkeeper like that one.

Jane Davis, Annette King's sister and a former inn-sitter, told Annette after dealing with some trying guests: "Now I understand why you talk to yourself so much. You're always saying under your breath the things you can't say to the guests."

The Freebies

These guests are not paying, but everything had better be right. For some reason, the most complaints seem to come from people who have a free or reduced rate for the night. We simply find these folks mysterious. You donate a night to a worthy cause. Someone buys it and gives the night to someone else. The someone else comes, takes one look at the room, and says it isn't what he or she wanted (or thought it would be, or whatever).

Cheerfully change the room, if you have another to offer. It just isn't worth the lining of your stomach to listen to the whining. Usually such a change satisfies them. Never refund the money—some of them are angling for that.

When the person who has won, purchased, or received a gift certificate for a free night tries to get a "refund," you might be so astonished that you won't be able to answer at first. For one thing, you should have a line on a gift certificate that says, "Not redeemable for cash." Explain that the person has won or has been given a night in the inn, not the money equivalent.

Many gift certificates are never redeemed. That's good, but it's also one reason you should include an expiration date on them. Some state consumer protection laws may require you to honor a gift certificate even beyond an expiration date; have your attorney check into this if you are concerned.

The Boors

Some guests simply take over. They don't always break your rules, but they will push them to the limit. Publishing your policies and then sticking to them is the best way to deal with this type of guest.

Hospitality is our business, and even when a guest seems rude or overbearing, we try to accommodate. We'll bend as far as we can to make something right or to try to make a guest happy. But we don't believe that our guests are always right.

Don't forget that you have other guests to consider. Most of your guests are strangers to one another, and it's important that these strangers get along in your house. This obliges you to be on your guard to weed out problem guests. If an ironclad rule is broken, you must firmly ask the guest to leave or take some other definitive action. As Heinz Haibach of Millstone Inn told us: "You cannot let them walk all over you. They must respect you and your house."

If you don't take charge, you can have the same problem Mae McQuade of Split-Pine Farmhouse had early on: "One novice guest broke all the rules except smoking. He came into the TV room within minutes of arrival and changed the channel I was listening to as I pressed some table linens in the kitchen nearby. When I offered to make him some tea or coffee, he insisted on coming into the kitchen. I waffled and moved the serving pieces I had set out for the morning. The other three in the party came down, and he joined them in the formal parlor. When I heard him tell them they could bring in their pizza from the car and use my microwave, the most I could manage was to agree to warm the pizza for them, insisting that they would have to eat it in the TV room and not on my white brocade upholstery. Now I have a copy of house rules that cover these points."

One clue to this abominable behavior is that this guest was a novice to B&Bs. Firmness at the outset in such a case is best. Letting a new guest have his way fosters bad habits that will follow him to other inns. Do those other innkeepers a favor and put your foot down.

Margaret Perry had some wedding guests at the Thomas Shepherd Inn who simply took over. Because her dining room did not accommodate the entire house, she asked guests to sign up for a time. These guests did, but then did not show up. They asked for coffee in their rooms at odd hours. On the second morning, they said they didn't want breakfast, but then came down and said they did. They smoked inside the house. All were discourteous. Margaret finally had had enough and told them, firmly, that their behavior was unacceptable. They straightened up after that, but they threatened to say bad things about her inn to others. If this happens to you, remind yourself that you wouldn't want them or their friends back again, anyway.

Courtesy is a basic right in an inn. Discourteous guests have to be defused or isolated, or they will ruin the atmosphere for others. Ninety-nine percent of our guests are courteous in the extreme. If they're around other people who are not, then we won't be doing our job.

If someone cancels a reservation after the established cancellation date and then tries to get out of paying, that person ought to go on your list of people who will always find the inn full. The reason is not revenge; it's to preserve the ambience of the house by keeping those who might spoil it away from the other guests. At the very least, you're going to resent them. You may think that you cannot afford to turn guests away, but in many ways you can't afford not to.

The Unreliables

These guests show up too early or too late. It's amazing how much this disturbs innkeepers. When you're new to the business, you think it doesn't matter when people arrive. Not true. You have many errands to run and much preparation to do, and it is just not conducive to a good experience for you or your guests to have someone arrive in the midst of confusion.

Many innkeepers will not show their inns to casual lookers if the rooms are not made up; we are among them. It just doesn't look good to have vacuum hoses tangled on the floor, sheets piled high, or cleaning carts sitting out. We all know it has to be done, but it spoils the illusion of the stage if you take the audience behind the scenery. It doesn't matter if the guest says, "Oh, we don't mind if the beds aren't made." You do. And that vacuum cleaner in the hallway may be an insurance liability.

Guests who arrive early should be politely but firmly told that you'll be glad to check them in at the time your brochure states, but before then you are busy preparing the inn so that their visit will be pleasant. They will ask if they may leave their luggage in the room; let them put it in the hall. If you let them in the house, they will want to look around, they will want a glass of water, they will want to use the bathroom, they will want to use the phone. . . . Pretty soon, you've lost half an hour.

Even if you have firmly informed your guests of your check-in policies, some people will assume that it's okay if they show up at noon or earlier, or at midnight or later. It isn't malice on their parts, or even spoiled willfulness; they simply don't think.

When this happens to you—and it will—don't lose your temper. Late-arriving guests know they have transgressed. You can still be polite, but firmly inform them that they have broken the rules of the house. With an early arrival, on the other hand, if the room was not occupied the night before, you may want to check the guest in. You can bend your own rules sometimes, but if you are a solo innkeeper/maid/desk clerk/gardener/marketer, keep in mind that as you check in this early-arriving guest, something else is not being accomplished.

One great technological innovation is the cell phone. At Biltmore Village Inn, we ask guests to call us a few minutes before they arrive so that we can be at the door to greet them. Knowing that your arriving guests can stay in touch—and they will do this for you—relieves one of the great uncertainties of the business. We suggest you use this technique; it will save you grief and keep you pleasant when you greet your guests.

The Weasels
Some guests may try to take advantage of your hospitality. A devious caller may book for two nights, as your minimum stay requires, with no real intention of staying both nights. Then he will tell you at the breakfast table in the morning that he must depart one day early because of "a death in the family" or "important matters at home." Others try to use gift certificates or discount offers when they are not valid.

With weasels, you must stand your ground. That's why you have policies—to protect your business interests. Don't accept transferred gift certificates, and don't refund deposits. If someone "must" leave early, it's the same as if they canceled after your cancellation period: They still owe. And you should collect.

Luckily, the devious guests are few and far between. Keep a healthy perspective, and don't punish the next unwitting guest with your leftover hostility.

HAVING ANSWERS AT THE READY
Have your answers at hand before you are confronted by difficult situations with guests. Most of our problems arise when we

are thrown a situation we have not thought about handling. Knowing that these things will happen and having your response prepared will relieve tension for you and for the guests.

Always refer to your policies, and keep them firmly in mind. When your policies are under fire, remember one important fact: Your inn has rights, and you must defend them. It is your business and your livelihood. This will give you backbone when it is necessary. The following example shows how to stick to your rules without alienating guests.

Your check-out time is 11 A.M. It is a Monday morning, and you have an empty house that evening. You are looking forward to your first free night in some time. You have four rooms of guests; three have left by 11. The other couple wants to know if, since there's no one in the house that night, they could check out later—say, 3 in the afternoon?

Your first reaction is to say yes. But you shouldn't; you will resent it. How do you tell them no without being rude? They are, in a way, paying you a compliment. They are also asking for free time.

Tell them they are welcome to the use of the public spaces and grounds, but that they will have to settle the bill and clear their things out of the room, because you often have walk-ins and you need to continue on the schedule you have set out. You don't *have* to give them any reasons; you're just being gracious in conceding them that much. Alternatively, you can simply say that checkout times are firm, and stick to it, or you can tell them that for a half-day rate, they are welcome to stay until 4 P.M.

When it comes to situations like this, think of yourself as the employee of the inn itself: Personify your business, and figure how you would answer to it if you waffle on policy. A partner can serve the same purpose, though it doesn't sound good to say, "My husband won't let me do that."

You do not have to explain why your policies are set as they are. You have thought them out and you have good reasons for them. You are not depriving any guest of anything that has been promised. The problem comes when you feel you have to take on the manner of a scolding parent to give yourself the backbone to enforce the rules. You don't; just be the friendly, understanding innkeeper who simply says how it is.

Guests will understand this. It makes them realize that your business is professionally run. And that is what you want them to think. You don't have to be rigid, and if you have no problem with making small changes in your rules, then you're being gracious. But if it's a real imposition, then you're just being foolish if you give in.

CORRECTING YOUR MISTAKES

Let's face it: Even the most experienced innkeepers screw up. Nothing feels worse, and we are all inclined to be defensive when we make mistakes. The first rule is always to correct the error as quickly and as graciously as possible.

Overbooking is the most heart-stopping of these errors. It happens at least once to everyone. You're filled for the weekend. A guest shows up, smiling—and he or she is not in your reservation book. You should immediately explain the problem and take the fault on yourself, even if it isn't your fault. Find a place, preferably in an area inn. If the other inn is more expensive, pay for the difference yourself. That creates goodwill.

You might have forgotten a special request, such as ordering roses or champagne for a birthday. Correct it quickly (and hope your florist is sympathetic). Absorb the charge yourself and tell the guest you will do so. Absorbing the charge has a couple of useful effects. One is to make the guest feel a little better. The other is to remind yourself in a painful way not to do it again.

You may quote a special rate or be running an online promotion and forget that you have done so. Leave a space on the reservation card for the rate quoted, and make sure that everyone who makes a reservation fills that out, especially if you change rates or vary rates during the week. But if the guest informs you that you have overcharged, don't argue. Make a little joke, and charge the amount the guest says.

A guest might inform you that her stay is a gift. You should know this when the reservation is taken, and you should have indicated on the gift certificate or its accompanying letter that the guest must bring the certificate along. There are two reasons for this. First, you don't want to have only their word for it (although you should have a corroborating list of gift certificates outstanding to check against). Second, you don't want a used gift certificate hanging around out there for someone else to pick up. Many inns write every gift certificate separately, with the names of the recipients and givers on the certificate.

You may occasionally have problems with smokers, although most now understand that inns limit the practice. If you detect a smoker coming in the door, make sure he knows you are a nonsmoking inn. You may have forgotten to inform him when the reservations were made. Explain that you may have made an error by not informing him, and ask if he has a problem with that policy. If he does, as courteously as possible find him a room elsewhere—even if it's at a Sheraton or Holiday Inn.

Carl and Dinie's Wedgwood Inns not only are nonsmoking, but they are smoke-free: no candles or incense allowed either. They've had too many close calls with in-room fire hazards. Your local fire marshal and insurance company will also applaud this. Biltmore Village Inn not only does not allow smoking in the rooms, but it does not allow smoking on the entire two-acre grounds. Guests who smoke can do so in their cars or down on the public street. Smoking guests have become very good about this.

We all have a responsibility as innkeepers to educate our guests. The effort you make now will save other innkeepers from having the same problems with them.

What constantly charms us is how understanding guests are, and how they will often go out of their way not to cause you problems—even when it might be your fault. They understand the fragility of your enterprise and know there are limits to what they can expect. If they like you and your inn, they'll do their best to be pleasant, just as you do.

10

Why You Don't Want to Be in This Alone

Innkeepers are remarkably helpful about helping other innkeepers, especially new ones. This is one of the great wonders of the business. Most small-business people are naturally wary about competitors. But in the inn business, although a few innkeepers might be jealous of potential competitors, most know that the more people who stay in area inns, the more business there will be for everyone. Under these circumstances, local, state, and national groups that work for the benefit of all their members have an important role to play in the success of new and established inns.

LOCAL ASSOCIATIONS

Local inn associations have sprung up wherever there is a significant concentration of inns. They serve a number of purposes, including matching new innkeepers with established ones for the purpose of mentoring. The principal focus of a group will change as the requirements of members and the area change. Focus fluctuates as inns change hands or as innkeepers drop out because they don't find the group useful any more.

Local associations have grown with the innkeeping business. They are now complex organizations with more varied missions than they used to have. You should remember, however, that the association is not the first priority of its members. Everyone has a business to run and possibly even an outside job. Time constraints severely limit what any member can do.

Ray Compton, innkeeper of Spring Bank in Frederick, Maryland, and former president of Inns of the Blue Ridge, says good associations do a lot for their members. They can offer joint marketing opportunities, set up member-guest referral systems, share operational business experiences, respond to legislative issues, and establish cooperative purchasing. They can also help keep innkeepers from becoming isolated.

"Working with other innkeepers in your area is important to create a public awareness of B&Bs," says Peg McCabe of the Queen Anne Inn in Newport, Rhode Island. "On a practical level, local innkeepers help each other with vacancy referral systems. As a group, we try to influence government decisions, like parking restrictions, that may impact inn business."

Associations don't always grant membership just because you establish an inn in a given area. Criteria for membership can include complying with local codes, demonstrating concern for guest health and safety, providing a common room for guests to congregate, meeting standards of appearance, maintaining a high standard of business ethics, and management living on the property. Membership is generally restricted to inns with a maximum of twenty rooms.

Most local associations provide some or all of the following benefits to their members. Each of these can be enormously helpful not only to the new innkeeper, but also to the ongoing inn operation that seeks to grow.

Camaraderie

The pioneers of the innkeeping business discovered early on the need to get together and remind themselves that they weren't alone. Innkeepers are generally gregarious people who enjoy groups. But they spend most of their time onstage with guests, who don't really want to hear about problems. Guests are, after all, on holiday. They want to believe that your life is idyllic.

Getting together with other innkeepers allows you to let your hair down and tell war stories. You can describe situations you'd like some feedback on, to see if you've handled them well and find out how you might have handled them differently. Often you just have a need to be recognized as something more than just "the innkeeper."

Camaraderie remains basic to such associations, and most require social contact with potential members before they will consider them for membership. That might seem nitpicking, but it isn't. We've all been in groups with an obstructive member (something about group dynamics seems to require that someone play this role). If a potential new member strikes someone in the group as obnoxious, even if the impression is false, then the group dynamic can be harmed.

Once your local association is established, you can share the common language and experiences that continually revalidate for you your choice of innkeeping as a profession. Greeting and dealing with strangers every day, nice as they are, doesn't substitute for the friendship of like-minded people. All home-based businesspeople have this lack of fellowship. Most nine-to-fivers have jobs at which they can rub shoulders with others who share the same problems. Innkeepers need the same kind of sharing, but the work and the schedule make this difficult. Only some effort to plan gatherings can overcome the scheduling difficulties. Some associations plan holiday dinners, gatherings on the porch of one or another member, or regular Sunday brunches (Sunday afternoon is often the quietest day of the week).

If a disaster happens, you'll be glad of these relationships. In 2004, Valerie Larrea, a single innkeeper for twelve years, had a fire in her carriage house. Other innkeepers immediately showed up to help rescue what could be rescued, take care of scheduled guests, and help with cleanup. "Everyone should have a disaster," she quips, "to find out what a wonderful support group you have."

Joint Marketing
Most members of groups will quickly agree that the major concrete accomplishment of a local association is joint marketing and promotion. This usually begins with the group putting out

its own print brochure or rack card and website. It's hard to overestimate the value of these.

Each member can have a reciprocal hyperlink to the association website from his or her own inn website. And the joint site will link to each inn. In addition, each inn can give out the group brochure (local, state, or both), giving it a wider distribution than any single innkeeper can manage. Whether or not it's fair, groups are often recognized as more legitimate than individual inns and can sometimes get media coverage that an individual inn, particularly a new one, wouldn't get.

As with all high-quality travel-planning information, inngoers and potential inn-goers save these brochures and bookmark these websites for a long time. Groups usually do not put prices in group brochures, because guests tend to think that a brochure is always current, even if they ought to know otherwise.

The expense of the group website and print brochure is spread among the member inns. Usually the group can take advantage of the economies of scale not available to individual inns. Groups usually print quite large quantities of these brochures—rarely less than 10,000—and thus can get a good price. It's a great value for members and a good example of balancing print and online marketing efforts

Joint advertising has the same advantages. Print magazines will give discounts on larger display ads, and members end up getting more exposure than they would as individual inns in the classified section.

Member Guest-Referral System

At busy times of the year, innkeepers can forget to refer guests on to other inns. More often, we refer them without knowing whether there are rooms available. Local associations can help smooth out this process.

In the simplest form of referral system, innkeepers take responsibility by turns for keeping up with the availability of rooms in all member inns. Each innkeeper must call in with a status report each week, or each day during very busy times.

The central dispatcher then rotates guests needing referrals through the list of inns with rooms available on a given night.

It usually isn't possible for such systems to operate much beyond a week ahead. It also depends on the individual innkeepers to keep the dispatcher up-to-date.

Some groups are more efficient than others at this, and there is clearly a maximum number of inns that can participate effectively. If the group's members are widely spread, it will not always be possible to persuade a guest to go fifty miles from their original intended destination. Referrals may not go to the next one up on the list; there is often some attempt to accommodate the guest's preferences for price range, amenities, location, and so on.

It is corrosive to the group for one member to accuse another of being unfair in handing out referrals, so most groups set up rules to prevent unfairness. Most often, however, members police themselves. If you treat someone else unfairly, then they will do the same to you. Pretty soon the association will fall apart or the offending member will be invited to leave.

More sophisticated referral systems involve revolving toll-free numbers. Telephone technology is such that moving a number from phone to phone is neither difficult nor unreasonably expensive. Still other associations require all their members to be part of an online reservation or availability network such as Webervations or InnRes. Each member inn updates its own availability, and an association-wide availability calendar is displayed to visitors of your group's website. Check out VisitBucks.com to view how it works for the Bucks County B&B/Inn Association of Pennsylvania and www.asheville bba.com to see how it works for the Asheville B&B Association.

Inn groups that use sophisticated telephone or fax systems or online association-wide reservation calendars are usually large and in very busy areas. Advances in technology are coming fast and furious, however, and every year brings new and interesting possibilities. With luck, your group will have members who are able to comprehend and adapt such developments for you. National and state professional associations should stay ahead of such developments and help their members, both individuals and groups, take advantage of them.

Sharing Operational Experiences

Just as we have shared a good deal of experience from innkeepers across the country, so your group will be a source of advice for those situations that we haven't covered or anticipated—and every week will bring something you've never thought you'd have to deal with. Sharing can help focus and solve a number of region-specific issues. You will also continue to need help, particularly, in the areas of marketing and promotion.

Group members are usually great at sharing ways of doing things. You're more likely to hear these tips at a group meeting. If you feel more comfortable working one-on-one, however, then feel free to call on individuals for advice in particular situations.

Responding to Legislative Issues

"All politics is local" goes the old politicians' saying, and it is true. When you combine a highly individualistic business like innkeeping with local politics, you have a recipe for frequent, and sometimes acrimonious, political conflict.

Some issues that come up will be local to your community; others will be statewide or national. The most important local issue is usually zoning. Zoning laws and regulations do not hold constant; if you are licensed under a zoning exception, that exception can be changed, although most communities embrace "grandfathering," the practice of continuing to allow operations to continue in the way they did before zoning was changed.

You may want to oppose or support particular zoning changes around you, and you will need help pressing your opinion in your community. These are highly political situations. City and county councils are made up of fellow citizens, with all their virtues and liabilities. They are not above being petty or shortsighted. A strong group will have political impact in those situations.

The other major local or state issues are health regulations, particularly those related to food preparation, and fire codes. Sometimes the enforcement of the regulations is at issue, other times the regulations themselves. A third area whose importance is increasing is the levying and distribution of hotel occupancy taxes, usually called "bed tax."

A strong association can help educate decision makers as to the advantages or disadvantages of regulatory changes affecting your business or community. If your association has (as it should) a political committee, those members should be well informed of looming issues and have recommendations for your group.

If, for example, your association has adopted standards for members, and those standards are stricter than the county or state requires, you may wish to press for the official standards to be raised. This will prevent substandard operations from coming into your area and spoiling the image you have established. Such operations will not be able to take advantage of the marketing you have done.

A recent example from Asheville is the attempt to establish a permit for bed and breakfasts in the city. Why, you might ask, would any of us ask for more regulation? There are several reasons. One is that a number of unregulated (illegal) establishments have popped up that are taking business away from legal ones. The association is concerned about the danger to the traveling public, and the additional danger that the reputation of good inns will suffer. The city needs to be able to tell potential innkeepers coming in what is required. The Asheville association created a model ordinance and met with the city to gain support of the planning and zoning department. The initiative met with encouragement, and we have every reason to hope that it will pass, although it will take time—possibly a long time.

The Asheville association has been so successful that the chamber of commerce has to remind its volunteer information desk workers from time to time that the Asheville Bed and

Breakfast Association does not represent *all* inns. But the association is now regularly consulted on any issue affecting inns in the city, and if it opposes an action, that action usually is not taken. That has a lot of value, even for those inns who are not members.

National issues are also important to you, and you can have impact on them. Your senators and representatives are not inaccessible, though you may need advice on how to get to them. Again, there is strength in numbers. Membership in a group will give you better clout and access than you have as an individual. If you are a representative of a business segment, such as tourism, you are going to get a hearing.

Cooperative Purchasing

To buy groceries for an inn of ten rooms or fewer, there's no reason to do more than go to the local supermarket. The same is true for most of your supplies. If your purchases are minimal, you won't have access to the volume discounts that can save you money. On top of that, there's some value in patronizing local vendors, if you can. How can you ask them for their business if you do not tender them yours? Though the thought may be distasteful to some, at times a monthly trek to a superstore like Wal-Mart may be sound advice.

But if you are larger, or if you can save more than a pittance on large items, then cooperative purchasing can be useful. Most groups don't succeed very well at this, because innkeepers don't like to lay out large amounts of money at one time. Then, too, someone has to accept responsibility for collecting the money and distributing the goods.

Some companies that specialize in working with hotels will provide the same group purchasing power to large inns. They will also do it for a group, if the group presents itself as a single entity. Sometimes this means that one inn has to be the "front" inn.

If your group is sufficiently organized to do this, you can save considerable amounts on large items such as refrigerators or vacuum cleaners. You can also save on items that you buy in quantity, such as linens, pillows, and lightbulbs.

This may conflict with the innkeepers' desire for individuality, however. Ripley and Owen, for example, much prefer choosing their own linens. And now that so many companies offer discounts and easy delivery, group purchasing is less attractive.

Establishing Standards

This subject will always be touchy for a group, which often is as social as it is professional. We usually find it hard to judge a neighbor, at least to the neighbor's face.

Setting standards is hard. Enforcing them is harder. At some point, however, groups are probably going to have to do this. They will probably concentrate most on standards that are fairly obvious and easy to get agreement on: cleanliness, adherence to local building and zoning codes, general comfort, presence of commons areas. In other words, the group will insist on certain minimums for membership, in order to give your group marketing some clout.

As far as rigorous standards are concerned, it is unlikely that a local group will take the lead. That has to be done by an outfit with much more distance from each member, so that hurt feelings won't cause permanent rifts among neighbors.

Early Warning of Business Problems or Opportunities

Local business problems and opportunities should be a major focus of local groups. Working spouses of innkeepers may have connections with area businesses, and the information they gather could be useful for the members of the group.

Opportunities often come up because your group is organized and known. Inn tours, for example, are quite popular as fund-raisers for charities. While bringing in money for the charity, they get the inns exposed to a wider audience. If you have confidence in your inn, you want as many potential guests as possible to come through. By concentrating them in a given two- or three-day period, you'll avoid the constant annoyance of the ringing doorbell.

Other opportunities might involve your group in business promotions for the area. The nature of these promotions depends on the concentration and geographical distribution of inns in your area. If your town has fifteen inns, then working with other merchants on a Valentine's Day promotion makes sense.

In addition to legislative issues, business problems for inns may involve the potential loss of clients. If, for example, there is talk of a major industrial plant leaving town, and its departure would cost you a chunk of your business traveler bookings, then you'll want to get your association involved with the chamber of commerce, service clubs, and other local businesses to try to persuade that company to stay.

Disadvantages of Groups

If you attended high school, then you know how groups operate. Every group seems to have the same cast of characters. Some members seem obstructive or unnecessarily picky. Some want the group to leap into projects without thinking, and others are so tentative that if they had their way, the group would never get anything done. Some members never voice an opinion, and others have an unequivocal position on every issue. Some seem to be taking a free ride, never doing their share of the work; others are in the middle of every project.

All of these behaviors may seem reasonable in other contexts, but in an inn group, they can drive you crazy. To your horror, you might even find yourself playing one of these roles.

Sometimes groups can use an outsider facilitator when they come to an impasse. Sometimes a group becomes so divided that members leave, either voluntarily or by invitation. Shakeups like this are difficult to deal with, but they often lead to a lessening of tension and a new resolve to work together.

One of the most difficult things for a group to handle is the spending of money. Inns so often operate on such a slim margin that innkeepers become naturally parsimonious about any expenditure. Add to that the rather intense independence of inn owners, and you have a natural formula for heated debate. We just don't like letting somebody else have a say in how we spend our money. Nevertheless, try to remember the reasons you joined the group to begin with. If you want the benefits of a group brochure and a website presence, you'll have to throw your fair share into the pot.

What we have observed over time is that the website is so valuable to the members that they will do anything to remain in the group. And that means it is less difficult to collect sufficient dues to promote that website.

STATE AND REGIONAL ASSOCIATIONS

These groups operate much like the local associations but concentrate more on marketing, standards, and political issues. They are often registered as lobbyists for the travel and hospitality industries. They also offer educational seminars to innkeepers to increase professionalism. The economies of scale offered by a statewide group make more ambitious undertakings possible.

State associations are still being formed. Not many are as well organized as the ones in California, Pennsylvania, North Carolina, and Virginia. Some states (Georgia, for example) don't have an association at all.

The youth of the industry is apparent as these larger organizations struggle to get organized. Innkeepers are very busy and always short of money, so the need to take two days off and spend $200 to attend a seminar when the benefits aren't clear tends to cut down on attendance.

But as Sally Palmer, former owner of the Palmer House in Oregon, says: "We're not currently working in concert to confront the challenges we face. We need to be able to reach consensus on certain issues. We have a lot of innkeepers who refuse to get involved with the organization because they don't want somebody else to tell them how to run their businesses. I think it's important to have as large and cohesive a group as possible. It's the only way we'll be able to deal with the overzealous regulatory bodies." The larger the group, the more clout it will have with legislative bodies, both state and national.

Another important function of statewide groups is, as Sally says, "to upgrade the image of the business. We have a wide variety of operations in this state that, like the hotel-motel industry, range from garbage to luxury. Unfortunately, the traveling public does not know how to differentiate among those accommodations. They go to places without reliable information. We have found that an unhappy B&B customer will generalize his bad experience across the whole industry, whereas a dissatisfied hotel or motel patron will simply avoid that particular establishment. We have had some scathing reviews about poor value. Associations that have an inspection process serve to upgrade the industry. People know they're going to have a nice experience."

Nancy Donaldson of the Old Yacht Club Inn in Santa Barbara, California, has been president of the Southern California Association. She verifies the value of standards: "One of our primary requirements of membership is that the inn be owner-operated. We think that's crucial. The owner must be actively involved with the day-to-day operation and in most cases is living on the premises." Inns must be inspected to become members. "One of the hardest parts is maintaining hospitality. There is a tremendous rate of burnout, and people just get plain tired." To help deal with this, the association offers seminars on burnout, one of the most popular seminar subjects of any regional or state association gathering.

NATIONAL AND PROFESSIONAL ASSOCIATIONS

There are just two principal national associations for the small inn business: the Select Registry, an invitation-only marketing group, and the Professional Association of Innkeepers International (PAII), which exists to professionalize the industry. Originally started by Norman Simpson with his guidebook, the Select Registry is now an association of inns with very high standards. PAII publishes a first-rate newsletter, *Innkeeping,* and provides seminars at locations across the country, surveys of the business, and discounts on services and publications. It is one of the best helps available to the beginning innkeeper. Your membership should begin before you buy your inn.

DON'T GO IT ALONE

You can also get assistance by joining and working with tourism boards, chambers of commerce, and visitors and welcome centers. Not many of them are going to be involved in the specifics of running an inn, but they will help you greatly with marketing and dealing with red tape.

The most important thing about participating in these groups is that they will provide support, advice, comfort, and guidance when you need it. Avoid the temptation to do things in isolation. You have to attend to such a welter of details to run your inn that you can easily neglect the lift you get from working with fellow innkeepers. Don't go it alone.

11

Taking Care of Yourself

"THE WORST DAY AT INNKEEPING IS BETTER THAN THE
BEST DAY AT A NINE-TO-FIVE JOB."
                                              —Carl Glassman

If the innkeeper is happy, the enthusiasm is contagious. It
spreads to staff and guests, and makes business better.

But because we spend most of our time thinking about the
needs of others, we often neglect ourselves. This is common
among caregiving professionals, and innkeepers can get stressed
out in the same way nurses often do.

Such work-related stress can have bad consequences for your
business. You can become short-tempered with your guests or
with your partner (and any innkeeper who says he or she has
never been short-tempered is a saint or a liar). You can begin to
regard your creation as a monster out to devour you.

You need breaks. But when you're struggling to achieve profitability, especially in the early years, you'll find it hard to close
down for several weeks at a time or pay an inn-sitter to keep
your doors open. You'll also tend to do what all vacationers do
if you do take one: play too hard.

You also tend to forget your age. Some innkeepers are young,
but many more are middle-aged or older. No matter how healthy
and energetic you are, you will slow down. You're on your feet
and on the go at an instant's notice and at all hours, so you can

easily overstress yourself physically. Renovation chores can give you repetitive-motion injuries. Strained backs, aching knee joints, and pulled ligaments are not uncommon. And you won't give yourself adequate time to recover.

Sam and Rita Rogers were in their fifties in 1986, when they opened the Melville House in Newport, Rhode Island. They find they are slowing down some. They compensate for it, says Rita, by closing "during the first six weeks of the year, our slowest time, to travel and visit family. We probably lose business in doing so, but it's a lifestyle decision that at our age is important to us, and we're prepared to pay the price."

There is no such thing as paid sick leave. Like other self-employed people, innkeepers typically work unless they literally can't get out of bed. Energetic people find it impossible to sit and rest when there are things to be done—and there are always things to be done in an inn.

BURNOUT

To see how easy it is to get burned out, let's go through a "typical" day for an innkeeper, keeping in mind that no two days are ever alike:

6:30 A.M.: Get up, dress, open up the inn, and begin breakfast preparations.

8:30–10:30: Serve breakfast and answer guest questions about what to do and where to go. Check out guests who are leaving. Get cleaning crew (if you have one) started on rooms. Answer calls about reservations. Update your online reservation calendar and reply to e-mail.

10:30–12: Make sure all check-out rooms are done. Write or e-mail reservation confirmation letters, and send out brochures in response to requests. Make shopping list.

12–1:30: Grab a little lunch. Take some cookies to the welcome center, and stop by the chamber of commerce to leave more brochures.

1:30–2:30: Do the grocery shopping and get back to the inn to freshen up for newly arriving guests.

2:30–3: Make sure rooms are ready for new guests and returnees. Check e-mail and meet briefly with a potential supplier making an unannounced sales call.

3–5: Greet new guests and begin setting up for afternoon tea. Make dinner reservations for guests. Bake a batch of cookies. Check the mail and your e-mail for brochure and reservation requests.

5–5:30: Finish setting up for tea. Welcome guests.

5:30–6:30: Serve tea and visit with guests—this is the fun part!

6:30–7:30: Begin breakfast setup. Eat leftovers from tea—it's your only dinner tonight. Do early preparation for breakfast. Take care of last-minute guest requests. Show three different walk-in couples around your inn. One couple books an overnight stay.

7:30–9: Attend meeting of downtown merchants' association on proposals for zoning changes. This is an important issue; you agree to be on a committee to study revisions (groan).

9–10:30: Total the day's receipts and prepare deposit slip. Close out your credit card processing machine. Pay bills and set them aside to be mailed. Pay other bills online. Answer brochure and reservation requests. Check e-mail one last time. Call your mother (you forgot to send her a birthday card). Greet guests returning from dinner and see if they need anything. Visit with them a little; this is when they're most relaxed and want to believe you are too.

10:30–11:30 P.M.: Take care of last-minute breakfast preparations. Set the table and make sure the dishes you need will be at hand. Check doors and tidy up public rooms. Turn off lights and button down. Head for a well-deserved seven hours of rest.

No two days are the same, but they fall into patterns. Try to get on a schedule for paying your bills, maybe once a week or twice a month. Consider online banking, or at least paying some routine bills via direct withdrawal from your bank. Some things ought to be done immediately, like answering reservation and brochure requests—they're your lifeblood. Other things, such as shopping, should be once-a-week tasks. Repairs and marketing efforts both can be constant. Even online marketing takes time to do it right.

You can see that with this kind of schedule, you'll be tempted to let some things go: exercise ("Climbing the stairs twenty times a day is plenty of exercise"), proper eating habits ("If it's going to go to waste, it might as well go to my waist"), time for yourself ("You mean *Friends* isn't still on Tuesday nights?"), and time for your family and friends ("I promise I won't miss little Amy's birthday next year").

Somehow you have to make it work for you. If you are lucky enough to have an iron constitution and a saint's disposition, you might be able to keep this up indefinitely. You'll delight in the awestruck reactions of guests who make the mistake of asking what you do all day (and they probably deserve to be told).

If, however, you're a normal person with a normal tolerance for work, you'll have to do something to stave off burnout. Spend some time thinking about and managing this challenge, just as you do others.

Burnout means different things to different people. Most describe it as a feeling of being trapped, of working harder and harder to get nowhere, of being short-tempered, of wishing you had yourself and your old life back. This condition slips up on innkeepers, usually about the fourth year. And it happens to the best.

Part of what causes burnout can be poor planning at the beginning and taking on more than you can really manage. But even the best planning can't head off burnout for the innkeeper who wants to create a perfect time for every guest. You can really kill yourself trying to do that. Owen often says that Ripley treats the guests better than their own mothers do; then he gets grouchy when they don't appreciate it.

Too much concern for your guests and not enough for yourself can result in burnout. You get to the point where you don't even want to see the guests. You find yourself unable to force yourself to your feet, or you wake up in the middle of the night in tears.

That happened to one of the best and most successful inn-keeping couples we know, John and Maureen Magee. For the first two years, they lived across the hall from the front desk. "I woke up crying at 2 A.M. in the second year," says Maureen. "I told John, 'You're married to the incredible shrinking innkeeper; all I do is innkeep or sleep.' It turned out that he felt the same way. We sat up all night, and we decided that the only way we could go on was to move out of the inn."

YOUR OWN QUARTERS

The crisis for the Magees worked out well. A neighbor offered them the house next door at an extremely reasonable price, and they bought it for themselves. Things have gone much better for them since. They have since sold their inn—on their terms, not because they were burned out.

Some hardy innkeepers manage to live in the middle of all the confusion of running an inn; all of us do to some extent. But the larger and busier your inn, the more important it is for you to create some place of your own away from the craziness. Otherwise, the sense of confinement that is a necessary part of innkeeping will come to seem like a prison.

There are ways to create your own quarters, and wise would-be innkeepers will consider this from the start. There may be spare space over the kitchen or a wing that you can keep for your own use. Later, you might convert that space to rooms, but don't do it at the start. You probably won't need that space at first. And by the time you need additional rooms, you should be able to think about better quarters for yourself.

Some industry observers have said that an inn isn't an inn if the owner-innkeeper doesn't live in it. And some municipalities require the innkeeper to be resident. You therefore have to balance your needs with the requirements of the law. If you live very close by—next door or in another building on the inn property—then in our book, you are still resident. If the legal requirement is so strict as to mean within the building itself, then you need to create—by adding on, if necessary and allowed—truly distinct quarters. You should have one floor or wing to yourself.

Having a place to retreat to, away from your partner as well as your guests, gives you an important sense of sanctuary. Guests will come looking for you, but at least you have that area for your own. Because Ripley is not at all happy about having people invade his kitchen or office, guests are told that the easiest way to get the innkeeper is to call the inn's number. The Biltmore Village Inn guestroom book explains that the innkeepers' day ends at 7 P.M., and guests are very good about respecting that. The inn also has a guest pantry with almost anything they might need in off hours: glasses, mugs, coffee, tea, water, soft drinks, wineglasses, and corkscrews. Such a guest pantry is a service to the guests, but it's also a great help for the innkeeper.

Innkeepers with children have to ensure sufficient sleeping and play areas for their families. "After living at the inn for the first seven years, we think having a separate house is wonderful," says Bea Briggs of the Bridgeton Inn in Upper Black Eddy, Pennsylvania. "We no longer have to get far away from the inn to play or to forget the hassles. A separate home [one block from the inn] has been perfect for raising our two children." Innkeepers since 1982, Bea and Charley attribute much of their long-term success to having moved out of the inn.

It's very difficult to run an inn or to raise a family; to do both simultaneously is nearly impossible. Decision point: Hire either a nanny to watch the children or an assistant innkeeper to staff the inn. Don't try to do it all yourself.

TIME OFF

You do need time away from your business, and this is hard to manage. If you're lucky and can afford it, you'll train assistant innkeepers who can be left with the inn. Then you won't have to worry (well, maybe a little). Early on, however, you just may not have the cash flow to support a salaried assistant.

This is where inn-sitters come in. Their rates and skills vary greatly, and so will your willingness to trust them. If you can find former innkeepers who have a wanderlust, you're in luck.

You can tell professional inn-sitters by the questions they ask. If they have little curiosity about the house or stand quietly listening without taking notes, you probably don't have the right person. A good inn-sitter should want to know as much as possible: how the phone is answered, what your policies are, where you keep the linens, what rooms have what kinds of linens and soaps, what amenities you offer, and on and on. A good inn-sitter will be looking to start a long-term relationship with you, so that repeat stays will be that much easier for both of you.

This service won't be cheap. You may have to pay a flat rate per day, expenses, and sometimes extra fees for extra work (such as making beds and doing laundry). Some inns offer an incentive, perhaps 10 percent of gross during the inn-sitting period, as an encouragement for the inn-sitter to try to keep rooms filled during the engagement. Good inn-sitters will keep a book on your inn or take your own operations manual to keep and study for the next time around.

You could also start an apprenticeship program. Aspiring innkeepers pay you to observe and help at first. As they gain experience, they can take over your inn by themselves for a week or so at a time. You can then pay them, maybe refunding what they paid you. The advantage to using apprentices is that you have trained these folks to do things your way. And you have seen them work, so you know you can leave your baby with them. The bad part is that you can do this only once with a trainee. If your apprentice is slow in getting her own place, you may be able to leave your inn with her more than once, but this isn't terribly likely.

Once you have the right inn-sitter or apprentice, enjoy your holiday and try not to think about the inn. Sometimes it's a good idea to arrange your vacation so that you can't be tempted to come back early. China may be a bit far, but a vacation in the Caribbean or Hawaii will do wonders for your perspective.

Breaks of at least a week's duration are important; you will relax and find different rhythms in that time. You will also begin to think about your inn in new ways, and fresh ideas and solutions will present themselves.

You might also look at your vacation as an opportunity to get inspiration from other places. Sam Walton, founder of Wal-Mart and one of the most successful retailers in America, loved to go into other stores. He went through them with a critical eye, not to find things wrong, but to find things that his own stores could do better. While you're away, you should pay attention to how hospitality is handled elsewhere. And take a tip from Mr. Sam: Look for good stuff you can copy and make your own.

Away from your inn and its immediate problems, you'll be better able to judge its strengths and weaknesses. This shouldn't contribute to burnout; it should actually revive your original enthusiasm and make your enterprise new for you again.

Just as you schedule maintenance for the inn's buildings, you have to schedule maintenance for yourself. If you don't, the business will suffer. In case you'd forgotten, you're important to its success.

PHYSICAL COMFORTS

It's not just your mental health you have to worry about. Innkeeping is rough on your body as well. Pay attention to the messages your body sends you. Take care of yourself.

Knees and Feet

You may think this is a silly suggestion, but it isn't: Get several pairs of orthopedic shoes. Spend the money to get good ones that look fairly good on your feet. You're going to be on them a lot, and if you gain a few extra pounds (almost inevitable), that weight is going to add to the weight on your knees and feet. Foot pain becomes leg pain becomes back pain, and all that leads to exhaustion. Most innkeepers say they'd rather have funny-looking footgear than aching feet and backs.

Back

Learn to lift and carry properly. You can make yourself into a beast of burden too easily, and there will come a point when you can do serious permanent injury. Backs suffer especially when you make beds and clean bathtubs; the stretch can really cause damage. Here's a little tip for tub cleaning: Cut off the handle of a sponge mop about halfway. It will allow you to reach to clean a tub without straining your back. Or get one of those squeegees for window cleaning; they do tubs quite well.

Stomach and Heart

You're going to have a lot of food temptations around, because you're tempting guests with cookies, breakfast breads, eggs, cheese, puff pastry, and any number of other cholesterol-, sugar-, and fat-rich goodies. Your guests indulge, go away happy, and diet later. You, however, are there all the time. You have to discipline yourself.

Consider the not unusual case of Ellen Thornber at Llewellyn Lodge in Lexington, Virginia, who gained fifty pounds in her first few years of innkeeping because she ate all the breakfast leftovers. Finally she decided to eat a bowl of cereal in the morning and nothing else; leftovers got dumped. You may hate to waste food, but your body has to come first. Don't feed the leftovers to your dog, either; he doesn't need a weight problem any more than you do.

If you prepare the same thing often enough, you might get sick of it and no longer be tempted. Try to keep some healthy snacks around, for the guests as well as yourself. Your guests will appreciate the gesture, and you will be helping yourself as well.

Exercise

You need some physical exertion besides the upstairs-downstairs bed-changing kind. Use your guests as an excuse to invest in an exercise bike, pool, or tennis court. Buy a corporate membership to a health club. Short of that, get outside and take a vigorous walk three times a week.

Appearance

Your appearance counts for something, not just because of the impression it makes on guests, but also because of the way it makes you feel. You need to treat yourself occasionally to something that makes you look better.

WORKING WITH YOUR PARTNER

Few inns operate as one-person businesses. Those that do quickly acquire a few trusted employees and advisers who often take near-partnership roles.

Couples that live together, work together, and make (and spend and lose) money together can find a whole lot of reasons to get a divorce. This is especially true when a couple buys an inn so that they can "do something together" to save a strained relationship. Couples have babies for the same reason, and usually with the same result: a quicker breakup.

A strained relationship will only get more strained by innkeeping. If it isn't strong, innkeeping won't make it stronger. In fact, it will exaggerate those traits in one partner that irritate the other. If one of you is methodical and deliberate, the other may find that maddening in the face of so much to be done. If one of you works quickly, the other may be angered by what seems to be a slapdash and poorly thought-out job.

Before you take on an inn, a long discussion about yourselves and your relationship is very much in order. A second very long discussion about the roles you will play in this endeavor is also in order.

Most potential innkeeping couples don't do this; they're afraid of what it will turn up. But it is far better to discover these things now than later, because, believe us, your strengths and weaknesses will show up very quickly. Even if you are totally honest with one another and yourselves, you are in for some surprises. You can't always accurately predict what you will actually do and what you are capable of doing, both good and bad.

Conversely, a good innkeeping experience can strengthen a good relationship. It produces a rare intimacy, which in turn fuels the fire of innkeeping. The Southard family—Regina, Jerry, and their daughter, Carol—operate the five-room Southard House in Austin, Texas. Jerry sees age and experience as making the transition into the business easier. "We were comfortable, very close, happy, and generally predictable as a couple," he says. "Moving 300 miles and buying the inn was a road of changes that was bumpy at times, but we knew ourselves and each other well. That has made the going easier."

Sid and Judy Clemmer, on the other hand, started the Leadville Country Inn with the usual assumptions about who would do what and found themselves wishing that they had been more structured about it. "I would have insisted—and this is hard for Sid and me—that we define our territories," says Judy. "We operate on totally different levels when we try to do something together. I knew that before we opened the inn, but I kept thinking it would work itself out. If I had it to do over again, I would define my areas and Sid would define his, and we would set a meeting time once a week when we would discuss things, but we wouldn't intrude on each other's responsibilities. The way things are now, there are constant differences about who has what territory."

They have tended to switch many of the roles they originally thought they would assume. "She's really the more outgoing of the two of us," Sid says, "and I thought that guest-greeting and all that would be in her area. As it turned out, I'm doing that more and more."

Judy has another interesting observation about the usual partnership arrangement of the small inn, where one partner works outside and the other takes care of the inn. She and Sid are both full-time innkeepers, and theirs is the only partnership in their inn group that does not have one partner working outside the business. "When one partner holds down a job away from the inn, that person is involved in innkeeping via remote control. They come home in the evening with barbed comments like, 'Why is that spiderweb up on the ceiling?' The other one, who's been dealing with inn problems all day, just flies off the handle."

These small explosions are very common. It's easy to be critical of things that aren't your responsibility. The partner who works outside the inn may have an easier time than the one who has to live with the inn. Ideally, the inn will begin to make enough money that both partners can be full-time innkeepers, but sometimes that doesn't happen.

Partners need breaks from the inn both together and apart. To avoid burnout, both major breaks, where you get out of town altogether, and minor breaks are necessary. Sometimes the outside partner feels comfortable enough to give the inside partner a weekend, or at least half a day, off. Remember, both of you need to get rid of the feeling that you are trapped.

Occasionally, you'll have to compromise with the standards you have set for yourself. You need to let out your resentment against the inn itself. If it seems like a "person" with its own rights, it can also become a personality capable of driving the innkeepers nuts. Once in a blue moon, leave the key under the mat for late-arriving guests, with directions to their room, and go off to dinner together with the cell phone turned off.

Here are some tips for partners beginning in business:

• Be honest with each other about your egos, emotions, capabilities, and motivation. Discuss your feelings with your partner. You cannot take shortcuts on these.

• You must have 100 percent faith in one another.

• Understand that all people have their own needs; be prepared to bite your tongue on the little things. Keep your eye on the main goal.

• Make a list of what you will be giving up personally— time, money, social life—and make a conscious decision to do so before entering the inn business.

• If you have children, of any age, talk to them about your new ideas. Tell them what you want to do and how it will affect them.

• Evaluate your finances. Can you afford this? Money woes can destroy relationships.

• Ask yourself whether you have enough energy and whether your health is good enough to stand the workload.

• Decide that everything you do will be high quality.

• Give each other space.

• Keep a sense of humor, especially about yourself.

Sex

Guests sometimes seem to look at innkeepers the way children look at teachers. They simply disappear when they aren't working. They certainly don't have private lives.

Guests may come knocking on your door at any time. This is one reason we recommend not showing guests your quarters, but instead giving them a phone number to call. The long hours and constant disruptions, not to mention heavy business worries, put a real squeeze on innkeepers' sex lives. When we talked to innkeepers about it, it turned out to be very much on their minds (and often nowhere else!). Most of our informants on this subject have preferred to remain anonymous. But they were candid.

Innkeepers are only human, and no matter how tidily we divide roles and responsibilities, there is still a tendency to bring problems into the bedroom. "Taking business duties home, for us a quarter-mile drive, can snuff out any romantic fires that have been set," says one innkeeper.

Is it possible to keep romantic fires burning while running a successful inn? Says one innkeeper from New Mexico, "Even though we live in a cottage on the inn grounds, it's hard to leave the business and light the candles." She candidly admits that it's difficult to have sex when they are under financial stress, "but the love is always there."

Is the entrepreneurial stress innkeepers feel any different from that in any other family-owned, home-based business? "Absolutely," says an innkeeping couple from Michigan. "As inn proprietors, we sleep with all our customers; they don't shop our store for ten minutes, make a purchase, and leave. Nor do we close our business at six o'clock and go home. We can't even get angry and have an argument with each other for fear a guest would hear us. Both arguments and lovemaking have to be scheduled around this round-the-clock business."

One unabashed innkeeper who always likes to be written about wanted to remain anonymous on this one (it may the only time in his life): "The joy of spontaneous sex is often impossible for an innkeeping couple."

A Minnesota innkeeper complains that residency at the business can present obstacles to intimate relations—particularly during the high season. "Sheer exhaustion from seemingly never-ending sixteen-hour days and the tension of sleeping with one foot on the ground and one ear to the wall can strain even the healthiest relationship."

An Arizona innkeeper who lives with her partner in a suite off the main hallway says, "We tend to collapse, from joy and exhaustion, the first night no guests are registered after a long stretch of full occupancy. Then we run around naked."

Dinie has another perspective on the subject. "I'm a morning person, so I tend to get up first to open the inn and start breakfast. Carl is by nature a night person, so he usually has late-night duties. These internal clocks are great for the business, but not the best for us. The inn has a life of its own, but so do we. And if we don't schedule time together, it's pretty easy to get trapped at the inn. Time flies whether or not you're having fun."

It is possible to keep the romantic fires burning. Some innkeeping couples "sleep around" in guest rooms at their own inns. Others escape to area hotels for R&R. Whatever your solution, it usually has to be thoughtfully planned.

Comfort yourself with the notion that an awful lot of cheerful hanky-panky is going on around you anyhow, and just join in with some of your own. Inns are supposed to be romantic places. As one Delaware innkeeper says, "I don't know how this Victorian frame building keeps from shaking off its foundation with all the rocking going on at my inn."

GETTING OUT

Most innkeepers just keep on ticking. We have met many folks between the ages of fifty and sixty who entered the field in the late 1970s and early 1980s and are still successful, happy innkeepers. It's speculation, of course, but we think that innkeepers are self-selected for endurance. They thrive on the kind of work that would bury most people.

Nevertheless, you will not live forever, and you will not be an innkeeper forever. You might as well start thinking now about how you will leave innkeeping so that you can lay the foundation for doing it as you go. We know it seems inappropriate to the romance of the venture to be thinking about this now, but as with a prenuptial agreement, if and when you need it, you'll be glad you made the effort.

As in any growth industry that has experienced rapid expansion over a relatively short period of time, a shakeout may occur in the inn industry. This happens when an oversupply (of rooms, in our case) meets reduced demand. Price wars often result as inns attempt to keep attracting new guests. Discounting of room rates cuts into profits; some establishments cannot afford it. Undercapitalized inns are particularly vulnerable.

This is the worst situation in which to sell an inn. When there's blood in the water, sharks show up. You're unlikely to get the price you need. Jerry Arndt, who spent many years as an insurance agent for innkeepers before retiring, saw this happen to many inns. "People paid top dollar for inns in New England, thinking the market would never go down." "Then they put a lot of money into their inns—everything they had. After September 11, business was down, they were struggling, and they couldn't sell because they would get less than they had put in." Not all inns were doing badly, but the marginal and undercapitalized inns that couldn't afford to wait things out were in deep trouble. "The farther south I went," Jerry says, "the happier the innkeepers were."

All of which is to say that the normal laws of economics apply to the inn business. Tacky of them, we know. Still, inns seem to have a resiliency. For one thing, they are often the innkeepers' homes. For another, more and more are opened only after the kind of careful research we're recommending that you do. We know of very few inns that have declared bankruptcy and closed.

Short-Term Sales
Aside from distress situations, there are some good reasons to sell in the short term. Here are several of them:

- *The fun is in the flip.* Some inn owners get their kicks from renovating and decorating historic buildings. Others thrive on the challenge of starting businesses from scratch. These owners get their satisfaction—and their profits—by selling turnkey operations. They often run their inns for less than two years.

• *Lack of money (and energy).* Undercapitalization is the major business cause of short-term sales as well as business failures. We've talked plenty about this above.

• *Lack of understanding of the inn business.* Many inn buyers, not familiar with the nature of the business, discover that their personalities are not suited for innkeeping. We hope that you have determined by now whether you are right for the job, so that you won't be in this category.

• *Personal reasons.* Some people fall "inn" love and drag an unwilling spouse along. Such couples often are already having problems, and owning an inn exacerbates them. This may happen even if the inn is successful. There are other personal reasons as well. Changing health or family circumstances (a new baby, perhaps, or aging parent who needs more care) can be incompatible with innkeeping. Some may miss their old jobs and want to go back to them. Others become lonely and want to move nearer to family and friends. Sometimes people just get an offer too good to refuse.

Selling a Mature Business

The sale of a mature business—longer than five years' ownership—is usually the result of personal reasons. Owners who have survived this long have already conquered most financial and business issues. In all likelihood, they have also come to grips with the innkeeping lifestyle and nature of the business. Their reasons might include the following:

• *Retirement.* Many innkeepers enter this business as a second or third career and are in their late fifties and early sixties. After five years or more, they are ready for—and entitled to—a retirement.

• *Boredom.* Most new innkeepers come into the business with new personal and business goals. These are often achieved after five or seven years. The excitement of building occupancy rates and creating a new life has given way to managing a successful but steady business. These folks sell because they are ready to change careers or seek new life goals.

• *Burnout.* Innkeepers who simply can't face repapering the inn, replacing all the linens and draperies, repainting the exterior, or making a major capital investment that has been deferred are just burned out. "Why sink $40,000 into a new slate roof if we're going to sell the inn soon?" they think. "We'll never get that money back in the sale price." This kind of thinking means the innkeepers have lost their energy to go on.

Sometimes an innkeeper wants to give up the day-to-day chores of running an inn without losing touch with his baby altogether. One way to do this is to sell to an employee or group of employees. A legal entity is created and an agreement drawn up so that ownership transfers gradually. This is good for retirement situations, in which the owner would like to keep getting income without having to pay huge capital-gains taxes. The devices to accomplish this are complicated and require lawyers and accountants to set up. It may well be worth it, though, particularly if you have built up considerable value in the business and equity in the real estate.

Moving On

After they leave the business, innkeepers have a number of destinations. There is no empirical data in this area, but our interviews have led us to a number of findings:

• Few innkeepers go back to their former jobs.

• Few face financial ruin. Even those innkeepers who had to sell earlier than they planned, and who did not yet have a profitable business, didn't necessarily face a financial crisis. On the contrary, equity in the real-estate value of the property may even return a short-term capital gain.

• Some, especially those who are over sixty-five, enter deep retirement.

• Some become inn-sitters. The need for itinerant innkeepers grows as our industry continues to expand. Many people are full-time professional inn-sitters. Some retired innkeepers go part-time, offering busy innkeepers time off for burnout prevention. Others become regular part-time employees at their former inns.

• Many turn avocations into vocations. They pursue new interests they developed while innkeeping—flea marketing, antique dealing, furniture restoration, real estate sales, crafts, interior decoration, catering.

Innkeepers seem to be adaptable, always finding and following new interests. In most cases, whatever they pursue afterward is as unconventional as innkeeping.

Index